Literary

Lust

ATRIA
BOOKS

1230 Avenue of the Americas
New York, NY 10020

ISBN-13: 978-0-7432-8827-9
ISBN-10:   0-7432-8827-0

First Atria Books hardcover edition February 2006

This book was conceived,
designed, and produced by:
THE IVY PRESS LIMITED
The Old Candlemakers, West Street,
Lewes, East Sussex, BN7 2NZ, UK.

CREATIVE DIRECTOR Peter Bridgewater
PUBLISHER Sophie Collins
EDITORIAL DIRECTOR Jason Hook
SENIOR PROJECT EDITOR Hazel Songhurst
ART DIRECTOR Karl Shanahan
DESIGNER Joanna Clinch
ILLUSTRATOR Sarah Young

1 3 5 7 9 10 8 6 4 2

ATRIA BOOKS is a trademark of Simon & Schuster, Inc.

Manufactured in China

For information about special discounts for bulk purchases,
please contact Simon & Schuster Special Sales at
1-800-456 6798 or business@simonandschuster.com.

STELLA HYDE

Literary
Lust

THE SEXIEST MOMENTS IN CLASSIC FICTION

ATRIA BOOKS

New York London Toronto Sydney

CONTENTS

Introduction 6

EARTHY ROMPS 8

Sin-liqe-unninni: *The Epic of Gilgamesh* 8

Homer: *The Odyssey* 12

Giovanni Boccaccio: *The Decameron* 16

Geoffrey Chaucer: *The Miller's Tale* 20

Geoffrey Chaucer: *The Merchant's Tale* 23

Anonymous: *Sir Gawain and the Green Knight* 26

Daniel Defoe: *The Fortunes and Misfortunes of the Famous Moll Flanders* 30

John Cleland: *Fanny Hill, or Memoirs of a Woman of Pleasure* 34

Henry Fielding: *The History of Tom Jones, a Foundling* 38

DRAMATIC INTERLUDE 42

William Shakespeare: *Romeo and Juliet* 42

William Wycherley: *The Country Wife* 46

EXOTICA 50

The Arabian Nights 50

Lady Murasaki Shikubu: *The Tale of Genji* 54

Sheikh Nefwazi: *The Perfumed Garden* 58

Bram Stoker: *Dracula* 62

Edgar Allan Poe: *Ligeia* 64

Ann Radcliffe: *The Mysteries of Udolpho* 66

~≈⌐√⌐.

CLASSICS 68

Jane Austen: *Pride and Prejudice* 68

Jane Austen: *Mansfield Park* 71

George Eliot: *The Mill on the Floss* 74

George Eliot: *Middlemarch* 77

Stendhal: *Scarlet and Black (The Red and the Black)* 80

Gustave Flaubert: *Madame Bovary* 84

Emily Brontë: *Wuthering Heights* 88

Leo Tolstoy: *Anna Karenina* 92

Thomas Hardy : *Tess of the d'Urbervilles* 94

MODERN 98

D. H. Lawrence: *Lady Chatterley's Lover* 98

D. H. Lawrence: *Women in Love* 104

Emile Zola: *Germinal* 108

Emile Zola: *Nana* 110

Colette: *Claudine at School* 112

F. Scott Fitzgerald: *The Great Gatsby* 114

Evelyn Waugh: *Brideshead Revisited* 116

Ernest Hemingway: *For Whom the Bell Tolls* 118

James Joyce: *Ulysses* 120

Further Reading 122

Index 126

Acknowledgments 128

INTRODUCTION

*E*VER wished you were Mr. Darcy? Or that your partner was? Is your Lady Jane looking for her John Thomas? The world is full of sex manuals that will allegedly bring the zing back to your love life, and airport bonkbusters designed to make you feel that you don't really deserve a love life as you haven't got a permatan, a six-pack, a luxury yacht, or silicon implants. *Literary Lust* is a much classier option. This is not boring pornography, but real literature, with plot and characters, and you can use it to spice up the bedroom action and polish your brain furniture at the same time.

This is not a book for the newcomer. We are counting on the fact that you have got past *The Cat in the Hat* stage (in literature *and* sex). There will not be a list of positions and how to achieve them; this is inspiration, a selection of the hotter scenes from classic literature from Chaucer to the twentieth century, with instructions on how to translate them from between the pages to between the sheets. You will have to be prepared for a little role-playing, but that should not be difficult for you—how often have you been Heathcliff or Connie Chatterley in the velvet recesses of your own mind?

Literary Lust is divided into five sections: Earthy Romps, Exotica, Classics, and Modern, with a Dramatic Interlude in the middle. A list of recommended reading at the end includes erotic poetry and some pointers toward modern writers whose work might inspire some improvisational role-playing for advanced readers.

Within each section there is a selection of inspirational book titles, each with its own entry, putting the work and its author in context, and pinpointing the outstanding parts. Quotes from the work establish the mood, the props you need are listed, and there is a helpful rating system (see below) indicating literary merit, degree of physical difficulty, amount of role-playing, and the level of lustful enjoyment you can expect.

THE RATING SYSTEM

LITERARY MERIT
A GOOD READ   UNPUTDOWNABLE   WELL-THUMBED CLASSIC

ROLE PLAYING
COME AS YOU ARE   LET'S PRETEND   DRAMA QUEEN

SEXUAL PLEASURE
♥ TRUE ROMANCE   ♥ BODICE RIPPER   HARDCORE

EXERTION LEVEL
☼ LANGUID   ● BREAK A SWEAT   ✷ ATHLETIC

EARTHY ROMPS

THE EPIC OF GILGAMESH

THE *Epic of Gilgamesh* was marked down on clay tablets about 3,000 years ago by the scribe Sin-liqe-unninni. He wrote it in Akkadian but was drawing on Sumerian tales that were ancient to him, so we are looking at a story that is more than 4,000 years old. It's probably the first literature in the world, so how fitting for this book that it is also well-stuffed with lust-drenched episodes. So Philip Larkin was wrong about when sexual intercourse began!

The action takes place in ancient Babylon (today's Iraq). Gilgamesh is the handsome, haughty, arrogant young king of Uruk. He can afford to be insufferable, as he is semi-divine: his father was the priest Lugalbanda and his mother the goddess Ninsun. However, the people find him intolerable and complain (discreetly) to the gods. The gods decide to make a companion for Gilgamesh, someone to balance his power. So the goddess Aruru creates Enkidu, a fully grown man, from a handful of clay, some divine spit, and a pinch of stardust. Enkidu is Nature Boy incarnate, all testosterone and hair. He lives in the forest, runs with the gazelles, drinks with the wild beasts, and sees off hunters. None of this endears him to the people or Gilgamesh, so a love-priestess (temple houri), called Shamkat, is sent to teach him the art of love and softness, and civilization, and also (for plot reasons) to inflame him with jealousy of Gilgamesh.

THE ENKIDU AND THE LOVE-PRIESTESS

The Enkidu is great for women whose men work away from home, or have gone rogue or retrosexual. The love-priestess comes to Enkidu as he is kneeling at the lake's rim drinking with the beasts. Reeds sigh in the background. She is soft and curvy, smells delicious, and is dressed in those floaty garments that look so delightful when wet. She bathes him, shaves him, combs his hair, and then they engage in a "rippling embrace" for several days. After that Enkidu gives up the wild life and moves to the palace.

So take your Enkidu on one of those into-the-wilds weekends and find a reed-lined lake, or turn up at the golf club (especially at the water hazard) and take him by surprise. Don't forget the soap. Make sure you are so deliciously gorgeous that he simply cannot resist, and don't simper, or play modest: you are an experienced love-priestess who knows exactly what she's doing. Take control. You might want to practice the shaving part on a balloon first to be on the safe side.

YOU WILL NEED

✿ A WETLAND ENVIRONMENT
(A LARGE BATH MAKES
A GOOD SUBSTITUTE)
✿ DIAPHANOUS GARMENTS
✿ A RAZOR
✿ SHAMPOO
✿ SOAP

✿

> "*For six days and seven nights Enkidu is erect.*
> *He takes Shamkat in a rippling embrace and*
> *pours himself into her.*"

INDOOR ENKIDU

If it's too cold to go wild, you can create the same scenario in your own bathroom, after your partner has come back from a hard day doing something unusually sweaty.

> "Bare your bosom. Open your legs. Show him your attractiveness. Be still. Don't pull away. Take in his scent. He will look at you and come to you. Loosen your dress. Let it fall to the ground. Let him lie with you. Do for him what women do for men."

📖 A GOOD READ (CHOOSE THE RIGHT TRANSLATION)   🏃🏃 LET'S PRETEND
💔 BODICE RIPPER   ⊙ BREAK A SWEAT (NOT FOR NONSWIMMERS)

THE ODYSSEY

THE *Odyssey* is one of the earliest masterpieces of the Western literary tradition. Probably written by the semi-legendary Greek poet Homer in the eighth century B.C., it is a sequel to the *Iliad*, and stars Odysseus, not so much a hero as a smooth-talking, wheeling and dealing survivor. When the story opens, Odysseus has been fighting the Trojan War for ten years, leaving his wife Penelope at home in his kingdom of Ithaca. Odysseus (and others) has angered the gods by destroying their temples in Troy. Athena is particularly peeved at Odysseus, once her favorite, and so she delays his return home with storms, temptations, mishaps, and misadventures. At least, that is what he tells Penelope.

During his ten-year detour, Odysseus has many adventures, romantic and otherwise, but returns in the end to the faithful Penelope, when he proves his love for her by seeing off all her oppressive suitors who presume him dead. We know this marriage is rock solid, because Odysseus himself built the marriage bed and it has a mighty oak tree growing through it.

Readers whose partners spend a lot of time on the road (salespersons, truckers, couriers, rock musicians, etc.) may find inspiration in the *Odyssey*. It provides a number of exciting lust games, but favorites must be Calypso's Cave and Odysseus and the Sirens.

YOU WILL NEED

✿ CAVE (CLOSET, DOME-SHAPED TENT, OR SMALL SHED WILL DO)
✿ WINE AND FRUITS
✿ FLOWERING PLANTS
✿ BANISTERS OR UPRIGHT POST, OR SEAGOING BOAT WITH MAST
✿ A FEATHER DUSTER AND ROPE
✿ MUSIC THAT MAKES YOU DISSOLVE
✿

CALYPSO'S CAVE

Odysseus lost his ship and all his crew when the gods created a great storm. Eventually he landed on Ogygia, the island home of the nymph Calypso. She fell in love with Odysseus, and kept him in her cave surrounded by a sacred grove of trees with flower gardens and fragrant herbs. Odysseus rejected her offer of immortality, but nonetheless managed to stay in the cave for seven years (you know how it is), a prisoner of luxury.

Why not make your own love cave? You could use potted plants to make a sacred grove around some little-used storage space. Fill it with fine food and wine, dress in a long silver robe with a golden belt, and lure your lover in. Every time he tries to leave, tie his ankles together with the belt and ply him with wine and honeyed figs. Don't go too far, or it may all end in a restraining order.

"For he had got tired of Calypso, and though he was forced to sleep with her in the cave by night, it was she, not he, that would have it so."

ODYSSEUS AND THE SIRENS

Sailing across the Aegean, Odysseus and his crew come across the island of the sirens. These are three beautiful winged women who sing such heart-meltingly seductive songs that sailors forget to haul on the mainsail and crash to their doom on treacherous rocks. Wily Odysseus gets over this by plugging his crew's ears with beeswax, then lashing himself to the mast. He instructs his men to tie his bonds tighter if he tries to break free. You see where this is leading?

Adapt this to drive your own Wandering One wild. If you have a boat, then you can go way more authentic, but stair banisters, or a stout post in the backyard (if the weather is fine), will do as well. Lash your lover to the "mast" and establish that the more he struggles, the tighter you will bind him. Then drive him mad. Use a feather duster to stroke seductively, as the sirens brushed their wingtips against Odysseus. Whisper dirty. Then untie him and have your way, or maybe even leave him tied up and have your way.

WELL-THUMBED CLASSIC (ANY TRANSLATION WILL DO)
COME AS YOU ARE (ALTHOUGH GRECIAN ROBES ARE MORE SEDUCTIVE)
HARDCORE ☀ LANGUID

"No one ever sailed past us without staying to
hear the enchanting sweetness of our song—
and he who listens will go on his way not
only charmed, but wiser…"

ANGEL OF THE MORNING

This is great for lovers who like to woo with their wit and blarney, and slip in and out of character. Alberto comes to Lisetta at night, stealing into her bedroom, but in a humble way. Then he must persuade her to yield to the angelic passion. Lisetta can take as long as she likes to be persuaded, and spin the game out for days. When she agrees, Alberto can get into character (and costume if desired) and make love to her. And, as no one knows how angels make love, now is your chance to try out moves that you would never consider in your earthly avatars. As the thrill comes from Alberto's transformation from humble monk to transcendent being, artistic types might like to smear on glittery gold or silver body rub; then when the monk's habit comes off, you will glow divinely in the dark. This can be a bit messy on the sheets. It would give things an extra resonance if you were on vacation in Venice when you try this out, but it's not essential. And there is no need to hide in a monastery afterward.

> "*He will disembody my soul, and set it in Paradise, entering himself into my body; and as long as he shall be with you, my soul will be in Paradise.*"

WELL-THUMBED CLASSIC
DRAMA QUEEN (DEPENDS HOW MUCH YOU LIKE DRESSING UP)
♥ BODICE RIPPER ☼ LANGUID (IT'S ALL IN THE TONGUE)

THE MILLER'S TALE

THE twenty-four *Canterbury Tales* make up the best-known work of Geoffrey Chaucer (c. 1346-1400). Assembled between 1386 and 1393, they are presented as on-the-road entertainment made for themselves by a disparate crowd of travelers on their way to the shrine of St. Thomas à Becket at Canterbury, England. Chaucer did his best to include pious, improving, and tragic tales, to suit the character of the teller, but naturally it is the bawdy ones that everyone remembers. Generations of English majors are routinely surprised by quite how filthy some of them are. *The Miller's Tale,* one of the lewdest, comes second after the uplifting *Knight's Tale.*

It is about an old carpenter married to a creamy young wench called Alisoun. She has two admirers: the parish clerk Absolom, who warbles love songs nightly under her window, sends her extravagant presents, and is rather fussy about his hair; and the student lodger Nicholas, smart, bold, and lecherous. Guess who she goes for? Nicholas, a student of astronomy and divination, devises a plan to make the carpenter believe that a Second Flood is coming and that he should spend the night sleeping in a tub tied to the rafters so that he can float away safely when devastation comes. This gives Nicholas and Alisoun all night to enjoy each other. It all ends in farce when Absolom gets involved, and Nicholas gets too smart for his own good. Butts are kissed and there are red hot pokers. (You don't want to know.)

YOU WILL NEED

✿ A GUITAR

✿ ASTRONOMICAL INSTRUMENTS (NICHOLAS HAS AN ASTROLABE, BUT YOU CAN UPGRADE TO A TELESCOPE)

✿ A BOLD ATTITUDE

✿

THE HANDY NICHOLAS

Chaucer calls his hero "hende Nicholas"—hende meaning handy, pleasant, and courteous. Nicholas's first action on seeing Alisoun is to grab her crotch and talk dirty. So the Handy Nicholas works well if you have not seen each other for a long time, or you are young and hot, or you are not comfortable with elaborate role-playing, or you are usually restrained and polite, and feel like busting out. Nicholas should not have it all his own way. Alisoun should toss her head and twist away from him (but not too strenuously; he should hold her "harde by the haunchbones"). Then Nicholas has to apologize and sweet-talk her into love. Alisoun sets the agenda for when they will meet, and Nicholas has to contrive a plan. The Handy Nicholas can be fun if you are staying away from home, and want to add excitement to the weekend.

> *"And prively he caught her by the queynte,*
> *And seyde, 'Ywis, but if ich have my wille.*
> *For deerne love of thee, lemman, I spille.'"*

THE FULL-ON NICHOLAS

Very ardent lovers might like to follow Chaucer to the letter. After they have made their plan, Nicholas kisses Alisoun passionately, but she has said no to full-on intercourse; so he plays frantically on his sawtrie (a small stringed instrument played by plucking) until he makes a melody. In other words, he jerks off. Why not vary it by having Alisoun do it for him?

> *"He kiste her sweete and taketh his sawtrie*
> *And playeth faste, and maketh melodie."*

📖 A GOOD READ   🤸 COME AS YOU ARE

❤️ BODICE RIPPER   ⭕ BREAK A SWEAT

THE MERCHANT'S TALE

THIS is the next-best-known bawdy episode from Chaucer's *Canterbury Tales*. It's a kind of upmarket version of *The Miller's Tale*, in which everyone stands a substantial number of rungs higher on the social ladder, but is just as lust-driven. Neither tale was invented by Chaucer—originality was considered a blemish on the rose of early medieval literature. Both are variants on a well-established theme of the old man, young wife, and a rapacious interloper. However, you don't need to have this kind of domestic setup to enjoy the style of arboreal love described in the tale.

Old but sexually rampant January, who wants to be looked after in his dotage, marries gorgeous young May, who wants a meal ticket. *Plus ça change*. January's squire, Damyan, burns with desire for May. He writes a love letter to her, puts it in a silk purse that he pins next to his heart, and takes to his bed, lovesick. January sends May to visit him, she finds the letter, and replies.

January has made a beautiful, secret, walled garden to which only he has the key. No one else is allowed in, or even to touch the key. (Metaphor, metaphor.) It is where he takes May for summer sessions of connubial bliss. Clever May secretly makes a wax impression of the key so that Damyan can make a copy. She sends the squire ahead when she knows she is up for some gardening with January, and he hides in the pear tree. So we have a secret walled

YOU WILL NEED

✿ A ROBUST FRUIT TREE
(PEAR FOR AUTHENTICITY)

✿ A SILK PURSE

✿ PEN AND INK

✿ A KEY

SAFETY TIP: LEAVE UNDERWEAR OFF
BEFORE CLIMBING THE TREE TO
AVOID FALLING OFF THE BRANCH
TRYING TO REMOVE IT.

✿

garden with a healthy young fruit tree thrusting up in the middle of it. Hmmm. May tells January how she longs for a taste of the luscious young pear she can see in the tree, but he is too old to climb up and get it for her, and anyway has been temporarily struck blind for plot reasons. But he helps May climb up there herself, and once in the tree, she and Damyan make up for lost time.

> "*And sodeynly anon this Damyan*
> *Gan pullen up the smok and in he throng.*"

THE PEAR TREE

Damyan and May first swap love letters and then pine for each other for months before they get together. Get into the mood by composing lecherous letters to each other and leaving them, in silk purses if you like, where they can only be found by you and your lover.

The Pear Tree requires access to an enclosed backyard with a fruit tree in it (don't be too obsessive about it being a pear tree— pears are not, after all, the only fruit). If you don't have a backyard, perhaps you could borrow a neighbor's (when they are out), or if you are really daring, go to a park, a botanical garden, or an out-of-town orchard. All the climbing and secrecy should get you both good and sweaty, and so when May follows Damyan into the tree, he just has to lift up her skirt and start thrusting. Fruit also makes a healthy postcoital snack.

> "*I moste han of the peres I see*
> *Or I moot dye, so soore longeth me*
> *To eten of the smale peres green.*"

📖 A GOOD READ   🏃🏃 LET'S PRETEND
💔 BODICE RIPPER   ☼ LANGUID (NOT FOR VERTIGO SUFFERERS)

SIR GAWAIN AND THE GREEN KNIGHT

WRITTEN by an unknown hand around the end of the fourteenth century, the long alliterative poem that is *Sir Gawain and the Green Knight* is one of the jewels of Middle English literature; it is also a wonderful adventure in deferred gratification and the resistance of almost irresistible temptation—and you know how exciting that can be.

The poem begins at the court of King Arthur, which is visited on Christmas Day by a mysterious and gigantic knight in green armor who throws down a challenge. He will allow one of Arthur's knights three tries at beheading him, on condition that the challenger seeks out the Green Knight in a year's time to offer up his own neck. (It's a knight thing.) Gawain, the noblest and purest of Arthur's knights, accepts and lops off the Green Knight's head, whereupon the knight picks it up, says "See you in a year's time," and rides away.

∼ MIND GAME ∼

YOU WILL NEED

✿ A THREE-DAY WINDOW IN YOUR AGENDA
✿ A LONG, GREEN GIRDLE
✿ WILLPOWER

✿

For lust purposes, this is just the MacGuffin to get the virtuous Gawain to the Green Knight's lair, somewhere in North Wales. Gawain arrives at a castle belonging to Sir Bertilak de Hautdesert. I will not be giving anything away if I tell you that this is the Green Knight in disguise. Bertilak promises Gawain that he will lead him to the Green Knight's chapel if Gawain will play a game with him. For three days, Bertilak will go out hunting and give whatever he catches to Gawain; and Gawain will rest in the castle ready for his big showdown, and give whatever he catches to Bertilak. Gawain—pure and virtuous, remember—agrees. For the next three days, Bertilak goes out hunting deer, boar, and fox. Meanwhile, every day his beautiful wife tries her utmost to seduce Gawain. All he will accept is chaste kisses, which he duly passes on to Bertilak, but on the third day he accepts the gift of her green girdle, which he doesn't hand over. When he finally goes to the Green Knight for the head-chopping stuff, he is saved by his virtue in having resisted the seductive wife, and just gets a small cut for the minor deceit of having accepted the girdle.

GAWAIN AND THE GREEN LADY

This is a three-day event. Book a short vacation somewhere wild, where there are woods and water. It will be more authentic if this can be at New Year, but not essential. Bring satin sheets and plenty of seductive food and drink. Take separate rooms.

A GOOD READ (ONLY IN TRANSLATION) 🕴🕴 LET'S PRETEND
🔥 HARDCORE ☼ LANGUID

DAY ONE

The man lies naked in his bed. The woman slips into the room, dressed in green; you know what turns your partner on, so adjust the clothes accordingly. Then she spends the whole day trying to seduce her lover. She can touch him, but he can't touch her. (She should pace herself, as she will have to push things on a notch the next day.) All he can do is pay her compliments and give her one kiss. He must not make her angry (this is not as easy as it sounds). At dinnertime, the game stops. They sleep apart.

DAY TWO

Same scenario. The woman must be determined, but the man must be even more determined. This time, she can win two kisses from him, but nothing more, however hot you are both feeling. Again, stop at dinnertime, even have dinner together, but sleep apart.

DAY THREE

You should both be feeling the full heat of restrained lust by now. The woman pulls out all the stops, and brings with her a green girdle—a long narrow piece of velvet or silk. She can wind this around any part of Gawain she likes, and he must let her but do nothing more than give her three kisses. You should stop at dinnertime and sleep apart.

DAY FOUR

On the fourth day in the poem, Gawain has to go off and face the Green Knight's axe. You need not do this; by now, you should both be so incandescent that you abandon the game and fall on each other. If you want to stay in period, the man can shift character and become Sir Bertilak, hot from the hunt and ready for action.

> *"The ladye luflych come lagande swete*
> *Felle over his fayre face, and fetly hym kissed."*

MOLL FLANDERS

DANIEL DEFOE'S breathless, action-packed, roller-coaster "autobiography" of its resourceful heroine Moll Flanders, was published in 1722. It takes us from her birth in prison as the child whose timely arrival saves her convict mother from the gallows, via gypsy abductors, the poorhouse, provincial respectability, the colonies, wealth, crime, prison, several marriages, poverty, even more liaisons, and countless children, to tranquil old age. After her heart is broken by her first love, she quickly realizes that what a girl needs and what a girl wants may not be the same thing, and takes the pragmatic approach to life, love, and men. Tina Turner would have respected her ("What's love got to do with it?"); Gloria Gaynor sang her famous signature tune ("I will survive").

YOU WILL NEED

✿ A HOUSEMAID'S APRON
✿ A FEATHER DUSTER
✿ EYEMASKS
✿ A SILK HANDKERCHIEF
✿ A THREE-CORNERED HAT
✿ TOY PISTOLS
✿ DRAWSTRING PURSES
✿ COINS AND NOTES
✿ GLITTERY JEWELRY
✿

∼ GIRL POWER ∼

Moll is a great morale booster if you are feeling a bit downtrodden or have been taking the doormat role in a relationship. It will inspire you to some very empowering role-play. The book is stuffed with sexual encounters, but very few descriptions of lust in action. Although Moll is astute, and full of practical advice on how to get a husband on your own terms, she does fall in love quite often and indulge her lovers, especially her lovely gentleman-thief from the north country.

∼ GET IT IN WRITING ∼

When Moll sets the bait for her third husband (treat them mean, don't be too available, respect yourself, get everything in writing—there's nothing *The Rules* could teach Moll), the couple stand in front of a windowpane and exchange flirtatious remarks, carved into the glass with a diamond ring. (Diamonds are forever.) If you

FANNY HILL

You could argue that John Cleland's *Fanny Hill* (1748–49) is not literature, but I would argue right back that as the Western tradition's original uber-bonkbuster, it deserves serious recognition. No one could say that Cleland did not warn them—the subtitle is *Memoirs of a Woman of Pleasure*. Although a bestseller, it did shock readers of the time (and this was the eighteenth century, when rowdy celebrations were practically compulsory). James Boswell, biographer of eminent literary figure Dr. Johnson, thought the novel was "most licentious and inflaming." Dr. Johnson himself made no comment.

YOU WILL NEED

✿ A CHAISE LONGUE
✿ LETTERS ON HAND-PRESSED AND SCENTED PAPER
✿ LOOSE ATTIRE

✿

∼ GET ON UP ∼

The story echoes *Tom Jones* (written around the same time, see page 38) and is a gloriously unreconstructed male fantasy. Fanny is an innocent, beautiful, orphaned girl who comes to London, stumbles artlessly into prostitution, has many adventures, and finally marries the love of her life, her first client. The story covers all the wholesome vices—straight sex, masturbation, fellatio, cunnilingus, girl-on-girl action (although it's made clear that this is not for our girl), voyeurism, group sex—and is written from Fanny's viewpoint. Cleland is one of the few men to describe sex from the female angle, and on the whole it is not too embarrassing, although Fanny always comes and is always ready, and Cleland provides most of his male characters with gigantic "machines." (And you thought James Brown had the copyright.)

"*Awakened, roused and touched to the heart, unable to contain myself, I threw my legs and arms about at random, lost in sweet transport.*"

WELL-THUMBED CLASSIC (BUT PERHAPS NOT FOR THE RIGHT REASONS)

COME AS YOU ARE   LET'S PRETEND

BODICE RIPPER   BREAK A SWEAT

~ VIRGIN TERRITORY ~

Fanny Hill is a great book for literary-lust virgins. In Fanny's first encounter, with her lovely Charles, Cleland teaches young hopefuls how to deflower a virgin. Later, Fanny and her colleagues are taught how to simulate virginity so that clients will pay extra. Yet it may also suit sophisticates who would like to remember their first time, and fancy playing virgins the way that Marie Antoinette fancied playing peasants.

Sexual activity crowds the pages, so there is plenty to choose from. There's a lot of sex by roaring log fires, by candlelight, in the bathtub, on a picnic, in a flat-bottomed boat; and many of Fanny's conquests come in uniform. There are even instructions on how to unlace corsets and slide off underclothes.

> "Crying out in my pleasure frenzy,
> I closed my eyes in the sweet death,
> spent with excess of pleasure."

FANNY AND WILL

Fanny is set up in a fine house by one of her serial lovers, Mr. H, a mature man of wealth and taste. However, he is not that discerning, as he employs the lusty, handsome young Will as go-between for his notes to Fanny, and Fanny decides she will seduce her own virgin. Great fun if you have a boy toy.

For this you will need several notes that can be passed between you, as foreplay. Fanny starts by "ripening" Will. Every time he comes in with a letter, she receives it lying on her chaise longue, clothes artfully loose. Every time he gives her a note, she makes sure their hands touch, their fingers mingle. When he is ready, she pulls him to her by his shirtsleeve, and places his hand on her breast (by now artlessly exposed). Act out these scenes and see where they lead.

> *"The sweet youth, overpowered with ecstasy, died away in my arms, melting in a flood that shot its genial warmth into the innermost recesses of my body, every conduit of which dedicated to that pleasure was on flow to mix with it."*

Tom Jones

Published in 1749, *The History of Tom Jones, a Foundling* is the masterwork of Henry Fielding, and was as much fun then as it is now. It is a fine example of the English picaresque (lovable yet slightly roguish protagonist has a series of adventures on the road of life) with a rich gallery of characters and a hero whom men like and women adore. Although believing himself to be a lowborn bastard, Tom has natural good manners, charm, grace, and gallantry, all the more irresistible for being artless and sincere. He is not afraid of declaring his love for the wise and beautiful Sophia. Plus he is described as very handsome. Men would do well to study the Tom Jones approach, as it is probably the nearest they are going to get to understanding what women want. (Clue: ardent bastard with no commitment issues.)

The story gallops over eighteen books, with a chatty, digressive narrator providing an entertaining voiceover. Wrongfully thrown out of his guardian's home, Tom pursues his great love, Sophia, to London, having many adventures on the way. In London, his beauty and wit do not go unnoticed and he somehow becomes a kept boy to the worldly Lady Bellaston. Eventually, after much confusion and confession, it emerges that Tom is really the son of his guardian's sister, and he gets to marry Sophia, and the result is a true union of wisdom and worth.

YOU WILL NEED

- ❀ A RURAL SETTING
- ❀ A STRONG LIBIDO
- ❀ EASILY REMOVABLE CLOTHES
- ❀ MASKS (OPTIONAL)
- ❀ INVITATIONS TO A SOCIAL GATHERING
- ❀ A READY WIT

> "*I am not used, madam,' said Jones, 'to submit to such sudden conquests; but as you have taken my heart by surprize, the rest of my body hath a right to follow; so you must pardon me if I resolve to attend you wherever you go.' He accompanied these words with some proper actions.*"

~ TOM, DICK, AND HARRIET ~

Tom Jones offers great role-playing ideas for both of you, although you will see that the woman does most of the tune-calling. Although the book exudes an atmosphere of constant high-spirited bawdiness, there are three pivotal scenes that you might like to try.

1) EAT ME

At the Upton Inn on the road to London, Tom dines with a voluptuous and slightly older woman, Mrs. Waters. They tear at flesh, sink their teeth into soft fruits, spill wine—you get the picture. Play "Eat Me" at a restaurant (maybe one with a hotel attached). The menu is pretty specific—big bowls of soup for lascivious spoon licking, lobster claws to suck on, beer, turkey, oysters, pears, and wine. Abandon yourselves until it's almost too late, then get a room.

2) GAMEKEEPER'S DAUGHTER

When Tom is an eager young man not yet twenty, he is seduced by Molly Seagrim, the gamekeeper's black-eyed daughter. This is an Arcadian interlude of honest rural lust; nature is ripe and ready to burst all around him, and so is Tom. The essence of Gamekeeper's Daughter is that Tom thinks he is the seducer, but it's knowing Molly who has set her cap and every other part of her person at him. Be forward and provocative, and don't be afraid of the obvious. Low-cut dress, wet T-shirt, the "there's something-in-my-eye" maneuver. It's Tom's job to let himself be seduced. Plenty of room for improvisation.

> *"He caught Molly in his arms, and embracing her tenderly before them all, swore he would murder the first man who offered to lay hold of her."*

---

3) LADY BELLASTON

When Tom arrives in London he meets Lady Bellaston, and the way she picks him out from the herd and hunts him down is an object lesson for Mrs. Robinsons everywhere. She sends him a mask and a ticket to a smart society masquerade. At the ball she makes her move and Tom is too gallant to spurn her advances. She teases him by leaving and saying that he must not follow her with such emphasis that even country Tom realizes what he is supposed to do.

The Lady Bellaston offers an excellent opportunity for women to polish up flirting skills that a long-term relationship has dulled. You can play this at home, with masks and everything, but it's a lot more fun at a real social event. The other guests should not know you are playing, and both of you can flirt with other people. Arrive separately, act as if you don't know each other, flirt intensely. Lady Bellaston leaves first; Tom follows.

📖 UNPUTDOWNABLE (1,000 PAGES OF ENTERTAINMENT)
🏃🏃 LET'S PRETEND 💔 BODICE RIPPER ⚙ BREAK A SWEAT

DRAMATIC INTERLUDE

ROMEO AND JULIET

THE best-known love story in the Western world, but none the worse for that. Star-crossed lovers meet across an unbridgeable social gulf, earth moves, boy marries girl, boy kills girl's cousin, then bungle and intrigue, and that ole devil plot device—delay—mean that lovers end up dead in each other's arms. Constantly retold and relocated, but still a winner. Actually, it wasn't new to Shakespeare either; he based his version (published in 1597 and first performed two years later) on a poem by Arthur Brooke written in 1562, and even then it was a well-known story.

You may think that R and J is only for the young, or at least the sprightly, especially Romeo, who has to do the balcony work. However, older lovers should not be deterred. Close reading of the text tells us that Romeo (practical as well as poetic) organized a ladder for his second visit to Juliet's room; it's supposed to be for Juliet to climb down, but you need not feel obligated to take things quite so literally. Nor do you need to actually go quite as far as drinking a potion that makes you appear dead for forty-two hours.

YOU WILL NEED

✿ A BALCONY OR WINDOW

✿ A GARDEN

✿ A LADDER OR REASONABLE LEVEL OF FITNESS

✿ A STARRY SUMMER NIGHT

✿

~ ROMEO ~

No guy is going to object to playing Romeo: he is a hot, young, street-fighting man with an irresistible line in lovestruck poetry. He and Juliet are kissing just fifteen lines after they have first set eyes on each other. Nor is Juliet a girlie pushover: she is as bold, impetuous, and witty as he, but she makes sure she gets a ring on her finger before yielding to passion.

The essence of Romeo and Juliet is their magnetic attraction; they can't stop looking at each other, touching each other, or thinking of each other; their love is all-absorbing. It takes you back to your first great passion, capturing exactly the way that the world stopped while you just stared at each other. Of course, it is impossible to go back there, but a bit of role-play may help you rediscover what it was that brought you together in the first place.

> "*Spread thy close curtain,*
> *love-performing night!*
> *That rude eyes may wink, and Romeo*
> *Leap to these arms,*
> *untalk'd of and unseen—*
> *Lovers can see to do their amorous rites*
> *By their own beauties:*"

BALCONY

Romeo and Juliet have already met and kissed at the ball, and Romeo has left his friends and climbed over the wall into the Capulet orchard to find his love. To play Balcony, Romeo must approach Juliet's house at night (the moon and stars and velvet night are essential background), and she opens her window, or balcony doors, to sigh about her new love. You can of course adjust this to your fitness level—it could be a first-floor window overlooking your garden. Balcony is a two-night game, so it's great for a weekend break. On the first night, Romeo climbs up to Juliet's room but stays outside; they talk and kiss and yearn until dawn, when Romeo leaves. He returns the next night and only then should you make love. In the play, the couple's passion is made more deliciously urgent because he is now on the run from the law, but this is not recommended.

"Wilt thou be gone? it is not yet near day:
It was the nightingale, and not the lark,
That pierc'd the fearful hollow of thine ear;
Nightly she sings on yon pomegranate tree:"

WELL-THUMBED CLASSIC LET'S PRETEND
♥ TRUE ROMANCE ✳ ATHLETIC (ESPECIALLY ROMEO)

*"My lips, two blushing pilgrims, ready stand
To smooth that rough touch with a tender kiss."*

THE COUNTRY WIFE

RESTORATION comedy hit the boards of England's newly reopened stages in the 1660s, as an antidote to the dour Cromwell years. Sophisticated, witty, cynical, and bawdy, it was written by gentlemen playwrights to reflect the worldly ambience of Charles II's court (he had at least five mistresses) and made great play with a new phenomenon: actresses; for the first time, real women with real bosoms could be seen on stage. Restoration characters have names loaded with innuendo (Lady Wishfort, Sir Fopling Flutter, Witwoud, Foible) and the plots were clever, intricate, and dealt almost exclusively with vanity, fornication, and the battle of the sexes. Not for the romantic, then.

YOU WILL NEED

✿ A CHINA CUPBOARD
OR DRESSER
✿ CROCKERY YOU
DON'T MIND BREAKING
✿ BOYS' CLOTHES
✿ A SHARP WIT

✿

～ ALL IN THE GAME ～

If you fancy yourselves as wits, you can have fun with any kind of Restoration comedy. Try *The Way of the World* (1700) by William Congreve for some high-class, Noel-Coward-style sexual banter between Mirabell and Millamant before they dwindle into married bliss. Or you could go for *The Beaux Stratagem* (1707) by George Farquhar which contains excellent tips on how to conduct a foursome with style and verve. The essence of the Restoration idiom is innocence corrupted, or in danger of corruption, with townspeople the embodiment of suave, villainous debauchery and the rural folk standing up for sincerity, true love, and decency.

> "When I think of my gallant,
> dear Mr. Horner, my hot fit comes,
> and I am all in a fever indeed; and,
> as in other fevers, my own chamber
> is tedious to me, and I would fain
> be removed to his."

~ COUNTRY STYLE ~

And this is what you get in *The Country Wife* by William Wycherley, produced and published in 1675, and considered raunchy at the time. The main character is Horner (chuckle, chuckle), a cynical libertine who has spread the rumor that he is a eunuch (you don't have to go this far) so that men trust their wives with him, and all the wives know he is a sure thing. (He was possibly modelled on actual cynical libertine John Wilmot, third Earl of Rochester, see page 123.) Ladies who visit Horner say that he takes them shopping for china, and sure enough, they always emerge from his chambers smiling, with china in their hands. Enter dull country husband Pinchwife. He knows something is going on but cannot, for plot reasons, discover what it is. To protect his stunning, young, apple-cheeked wife Margery, and save her virtue in the wicked city, he dresses her in boys' clothes. This fools no one, and the minute she sees Horner, she too wants to discuss bone china with him in his cupboard.

EXOTICA

THE ARABIAN NIGHTS

Also known as *A Thousand Nights and One Night* (*alf laylah wa laylah* in Arabic), *The Arabian Nights* is a collection of Persian, Arabic, and Indian folktales handed down through several centuries; Scheherazade (see below) first gets a name-check in the ninth century A.D. (as Shîrâzâd). No definitive text exists, but there are various different manuscripts and they all include classics such as *Ali Baba*, *Aladdin*, and *Sinbad*, and most of the basic plotlines in Western literature. The work first became known in the West via the translation into French by Antoine Galland in 1704–05. Naturally, the indefatigable orientalist Sir Richard Burton made a version between 1885–88, just after he had finished the *Kama Sutra* (1883) and while he was at work on his first version of *The Perfumed Garden* (see page 58).

YOU WILL NEED

✿ A SOFA OR DIVAN
✿ A LARGE BATH, WITH SENSUAL OILS AND ESSENCES
✿ WINE
✿ POMEGRANATES, FIGS, STRAWBERRIES
✿ ARABIC-STYLE GARMENTS

✿

～ REVENGE ～

The stories in *The Arabian Nights* are told by Scheherazade, the beautiful and intelligent daughter of the Grand Vizier. The Sultan, having been deceived by his first wife, has found a very satisfying way of revenging himself on all women: he marries a bride every day and has her beheaded in the morning after their wedding night. Scheherazade volunteers to be a bride, and then cleverly keeps her head by telling the Sultan a ripping yarn every night, but stopping at the cliff-hanger moment because it's time for her execution. The Sultan reprieves her until he hears the end of the story, then she starts a new one. Clever, eh? At the end of three years' hard yarn-spinning, Scheherazade has three children by the Sultan, and he has fallen in love with her and forgiven womankind.

THE TALE OF GENJI

Claimed as the first novel in literature, *The Tale of Genji* was written in Heian Period Japan (around the eleventh century) by Lady Murasaki Shikubu, but is set in what was the distant past for her. It does not have a coherent narrative or an intriguing plotline, just self-contained episodes running chronologically. There are fifty-four chapters, or stories, arranged over three sections.

For lust purposes, the most interesting are the first thirty-three, from the birth of Hikaru Genji, the Shining Prince, via the many liaisons and marriages of his vigorous youth, to late middle age. Genji is the son of the emperor and his most beautiful concubine, and is, of course, irresistibly handsome and magnetically charming, yet slightly outside society, like an early Japanese Tom Jones. Genji falls in and out of love hard and often. He spends a lot of his youth chasing after women he can't have (his stepmother, other men's wives, ladies from enemy-court factions, women above or below his station), showering them with plaintive poems, and sliding in and out of perfumed, draped spaces under cover of the night.

YOU WILL NEED

✿ CALLIGRAPHY PENS AND COLORED PAPER TO WRITE MESSAGES AND POEMS
✿ A SILK CLOAK (IMPROVISE WITH A SHEET IF NECESSARY)
✿ YOUR SIGNATURE PERFUME (BOTH)
✿ KIMONOS AND FANS (FOR BOTH)
✿ A GO SET (A TRADITIONAL EAST ASIAN BOARD GAME)
✿

There are many Genji games to choose from, but in each, Genji is always the ardent lover and persistent poet; the lady can be demure, reticent, forthright, cross, keen, or rather distant, at least to his face. A good place to start is The Shell of the Locust, the story of Genji and Utsusemi, the young wife of the Governor of Iyo.

"*I yearn to dream again the dream of that night.
The nights go by in lonely wakefulness.
There are no nights of sleep.*"

GOVERNOR'S WIFE

This is very good for lovers who find it difficult to express their feelings, or say the l-word out loud. There is hardly any need to talk; Genji sends enigmatic poems and love notes to Utsusemi, then creeps into her room at night, picks her up in his arms, and takes her to his own bed. In the morning you should part in silence, but write each other more poems, telling each other how it was for you. Keep writing notes for as long as you like. This is a two-part game, and Genji returns the following night, or a few nights later. This time, Utsusemi smells his scented robes as he comes in, and slips out and away, leaving only her silken cloak, her "shell," which he steals and wraps around himself.

> ## "Beneath a tree, a locust's empty shell. Sadly I muse upon the shell of a lady."

In the story, Utsusemi leaves her gorgeous young stepdaughter sleeping in her bed, and Genji, rather ungallantly (he is a young man), makes vows of love to her. Obviously, you cannot do this, but Utsusemi could play two parts—slipping away as the reticent, demure, governor's wife, and reappearing as the altogether more robust and passionate stepdaughter. Just a thought.

📖 A GOOD READ (IN THE RIGHT TRANSLATION) 👯 LET'S PRETEND
♥ TRUE ROMANCE ☼ LANGUID

Many chapters are named for flowers or trees, so you could scatter your bed with appropriate blossoms for the game. You might also consider investing in some shunga images (*shunga* means images of springtime, and spring has an undercurrent of thrusting vigorous lust; shunga rolls were used as sex manuals by young men and given to newlyweds as presents.) Another atmospheric prop would be a Go set (the East Asian board game), to play when all passion is spent.

"Naturally soft and pliant, she was suddenly firm. It was as with the young bamboo: she bent but was not to be broken."

THE PERFUMED GARDEN

Translated into French by an army officer who discovered the original Arabic manuscript in Algiers, *The Perfumed Garden for the Soul's Recreation* (*Er Roud el ater p'nezaha el Khaterr*) is a nineteenth-century sex manual written by Sheikh Nefwazi. While paying homage to the *Kama Sutra* (not included in this book because it lacks narrative and characterization), it is a work of wit and charm, full of anecdotes, stories, and legends, as well as the eleven basic positions, twenty-five variations, a guide to kissing, how to give good foreplay, an essay on why size really matters and what to do about it, tips on how to make love if either of you has a physical problem, lists of descriptive nicknames given to the penis and vagina, and lots of sound advice on when, how, where, and with whom to copulate.

YOU WILL NEED

✿ A GOLDEN ROBE (OR DESIRABLE DESIGNER GARMENT)
✿ REFRESHMENTS (E.G. FIGS, HONEY, POMEGRANATES, MINT TEA)
✿ A LUXURIOUS DAYBED
✿ A SILK HANDKERCHIEF

✿

~ BURTON AGAIN ~

The first printed edition was published in Paris, naturally, in 1886. Sir Richard Burton (remember him from page 50?) lost no time in translating it into English. Unsatisfied with the first version, so he claimed, he started on another translation two years later; he had still not finished it when he died aged sixty-nine (how very appropriate) in 1890; his widow Isabella promptly burned the new version and all his notes.

∼ HAMDONNA AND BAHLOUL ∼

One of the many stories in *The Perfumed Garden* concerns Hamdonna and Bahloul. Hamdonna is the beautiful daughter of the Sultan Mamoum, and the wife of the Grand Vizier, so this scenario panders to every girl's inner princess. Bahloul is the cunning court jester and a ladies' man, who is much smarter than he appears.

Bahloul's wit earns him a present from the Sultan, a beautiful golden robe, which Hamdonna wants as soon as she sees it. She summons Bahloul to her room, and demands the robe, but he will only give it to her if she will have sex with him. He is so persuasive that they make love three times, and he still ends up keeping the robe.

GOLDEN ROBE

Experienced couples that enjoy mind games, light teasing, and high-grade dirty talk will enjoy Golden Robe. The ostensible object is to win the robe. (If you don't have such a thing, any desirable designer garment will do.) Always start in the same way, then add your own flourishes and variations. Bahloul puts on the object of desire, and Hamdonna invites him in, and offers refreshments.

> "Here we have the ruin of all women and the cause of many troubles. O Bahloul! I never saw a more beautiful dart than yours!"

WELL-THUMBED CLASSIC · LET'S PRETEND · HARDCORE

BREAK A SWEAT (HIGH STAMINA NEEDED)

1) TALK TALK

Hamdonna tries to cajole the robe out of Bahloul. Now is the chance for some high-class dirty talking. Bahloul says he can only give up the robe to the one he has made love to, and tells Hamdonna (in verse if you're really smart) how good he is at it, how much he wants her, how gorgeous and willing his member is, and how he can do it more than once. Spend as long as you like doing this, until Hamdonna is melting and Bahloul is stiff.

2) A LITTLE LESS CONVERSATION

Hamdonna pulls him onto her silken couch, trying to slip him out of the robe. Bahloul must remain in control, and refuse to take it off until his desire is satisfied. He must insist that she goes on top (make up your own excuse—he says his loins hurt). Afterward, as she mops them down with a silk handkerchief, he still refuses to give her the robe—she has had a free ride, and should not expect to be repaid.

3) A LITTLE MORE ACTION

Hamdonna takes off her clothes and lures Bahloul back; this time he rides her. When they have finished, he still refuses to give her the robe; they are just quits now, and she must play once more for the robe.

4) WINNER TAKES ALL

At last, he takes it off, folds it, and gives it to her; in return, she invites him to do what he likes with her.

DRACULA

A MILLION-SELLER in its day (1897), *Dracula* was Bram Stoker's one-hit blockbuster. Written in the form of letters, journals, diaries, and telegrams, a structure you'd think would make it a rather chilly, cerebral affair, it oozes lust and sex (and blood). The story has a visceral grip from the start: we are barely halfway into Chapter Three before mild-mannered, newly engaged solicitor Jonathan Harker is lured to Castle Dracula for some dubious real-estate conveyancing, and is almost undone by three terrible, beautiful vampires.

You know the story (cursed immortal's insatiable desire for fresh blood)—it's been filmed obsessively—but read the book anyway for its seductive atmosphere of languid voluptuousness with a dark edge. Although no sexual encounter is actually described, Stoker is great at evoking the altered states that desire brings, the obsessive focus on the lust object before sex, and the languid, dreamy, heavy-limbed, out-of-body sensation afterward. Any game will be successful against this background.

YOU WILL NEED

✿ A FLOPPY WHITE SHIRT
✿ A VERY TIGHT BUSTIER
✿ CANDLES
✿ FAKE BLOOD (OPTIONAL)
✿ VERY RED LIPSTICK.
✿ LONG, BLACK CAPE
✿ HEAVY SCENT
✿

> *"I closed my eyes in a languorous ecstasy and waited—waited with beating heart."*

WELL-THUMBED CLASSIC　　DRAMA QUEEN
BODICE RIPPER　　LANGUID

VAMPYRA

Of course, you can only play Vampyra at night, and it takes quite a lot of set-dressing (candles, incense, heavy drapes, optional fake blood) and costumery. It's great for extrovert girls who love introvert boys who find it hard to initiate. Jonathan Harker lies on the bed, half-asleep; he plays helpless throughout. Vampyra wears something tight and low-cut, blood-red lipstick, and heavy scent. (Keep this scent just for the game; then every time you catch a whiff, you will be transported.) Vampyra seduces Jonathan any way that she likes, but the first kiss is always to the throat. If you enjoy the game, reverse the roles, with Vampyra as the doomed Lucy Westenra and Jonathan as the Count.

THE MYSTERIES OF UDOLPHO

MIXING long descriptive passages, poetry, horror, suspense, romance, ruined castles, evil aristocrats, bandits, stainless heroes, and the kind of plotlines modern soap operas would grab with both hands, the three-volume Gothic novel always starred a breathless young heroine, and was adored by breathless young middle-class ladies who had hours of enforced leisure to fill. The queen of what is now an almost unreadable genre was Mrs. Ann Radcliffe, and *The Mysteries of Udolpho* (1794) was her triumph. Beautiful Emily St. Aubert loves the Chevalier Valancourt, but she is whisked away from him by a murderous step-uncle, and has to stay in horrid Castle Udolpho until Volume III (an awful lot of pages later) when the lovers are reunited. There are not many sex scenes, but the febrile atmosphere and emotional intensity that drenches every page can inspire those who enjoy dominant/submissive games, but would like to give them some class and style.

YOU WILL NEED

✿ MANACLES (VELVET-LINED) OR CHAINS

✿ A ROBUST CHAIR, IRON BEDSTEAD, OR ACCESS TO A DUNGEON

✿

RESCUE ME

While wandering around the brooding corridors of Castle Udolpho looking for Valancourt, Emily comes across dungeons and a chair with manacles, and shivers deliciously at the thought of the tortures it has seen. Rescue Me is a classic maiden-in-peril scenario. Emily must be tied to a chair or the bed by the wicked Count Montini, and then Valancourt bounds to the rescue. (Double up the roles for more fun.)

She need not be freed straight away—Valancourt can spend some time in protestations of love, with appropriate actions. The whole idea is to have fun, but always have a get-out password for these sorts of games.

"*Emily I have loved you—I do love you— better than my life!*"

WELL-THUMBED CLASSIC (A VERY LONG VACATION READ)

LET'S PRETEND HARDCORE

LANGUID (FOR EMILY) BREAK A SWEAT (FOR VALANCOURT)

Classics

Pride and Prejudice

It is a truth universally acknowledged that Jane Austen's second novel provides the template for practically every love story written since it was published in 1813 (seventeen years after she wrote it). Boy meets girl, instant mutual antagonism, misunderstandings, misrepresentations, mistimings, heroic action, mutual adoration, happy ever after. Easy.

～ ADMIRABLE RESTRAINT ～

The difference between Austen and modern romancers is sex. Some people will tell you that there is no sex in Austen's oeuvre, but that is because they are careless readers. When Darcy and Elizabeth meet unexpectedly at Pemberley, both are so overcome with desire that she can't speak, and he gibbers meaninglessly. Austen lust is all about restraint, pleasure postponed, the quivering deliciousness of unconsummated desire; and when you remember that the standard costume for an Austen heroine has her bosoms displayed on an eye-level shelf, and gentlemen have to conceal the gun in their pocket while laced into tight breeches, you will appreciate their self-discipline even more.

YOU WILL NEED

✿ A COUNTRY ESTATE
(OR SIMILAR)
✿ RESTRAINT
✿ AN IRONIC WIT

✿

PEMBERLEY

There are two ways to play this: only meet in the company of others, so that you are constantly chaperoned until you can't wait to be alone together again; or take long country walks together without speaking much. It's even better if you set off on LCWS separately, and bump into each other on the way, but make sure you take a map in case of poor navigation.

It's unlikely that either of you will have a vast country estate like Darcy's Pemberley, so improvise with parks, grand houses open to the public, etc. (the presence of tour guides and security guards will intensify the need for restraint). City-dwellers might try this at museums or art galleries. You meet, blush, and speak of the weather, and steal sidelong glances when the other isn't looking. Leave separately and don't meet again for a week, if you can bear it.

"*In vain have I struggled.*
It will not do. My feelings
will not be repressed.
You must allow me to tell
you how ardently I admire
and love you."

WELL-THUMBED CLASSIC   LET'S PRETEND
♥ TRUE ROMANCE   ☼ LANGUID

MANSFIELD PARK

CONSIDERED Jane Austen's most "difficult" book, *Mansfield Park* (1811–13) features the very dull heroine Fanny Price, who sits still in the middle of it, emitting super-delicate sensibility. Around her, however, is a whirligig of thwarted passion, bad behavior, elopement, and adultery, so there is plenty of scope for lust. (Fanny herself is steadfastly in love with her cousin Edmund Bertram, but does nothing about it other than sitting on her hands for eight years and waiting for him to appreciate her solid worth, so she is not really an inspiration unless you are up for a really long game.) The sexual threat (or promise) is generated by the interloping Crawfords, a rich, careless, and cosmopolitan brother-and-sister act, who swoop down on the rural repose of Mansfield Park like golden eagles onto a flock of sheep.

YOU WILL NEED

✿ GREEN BAIZE DRAPES
✿ SPACE FOR A SMALL STAGE
✿ A GOOD MEMORY FOR LINES
✿ AN AMATEUR THEATER
GROUP (START YOUR OWN
IF NECESSARY)

✿

Henry Crawford is one of literature's most delicious, irresistible, charming bastards, and his sister Mary is a gorgeous, clever butterfly with ice in her heart. Henry homes in on all the young women of Mansfield, and Mary corrals Edmund, the upright younger son. On an outing to Sotherton, the home of Maria Bertram's doltish intended, Henry persuades Maria to slip with him through the bars of the iron fence and out into the wilderness while her betrothed fetches the key to the legitimate gate. Fanny fears they will fall into the ha-ha, a type of ditch invisible from the great house. Make of that what metaphorical hay you will. Outdoor types might like to play Ha Ha while visiting stately homes, but not with each other's fiancé(e)s.

STAGE STRUCK

The most fun inspiration (as well as significant plot hinge) in *Mansfield Park* is the theatricals. Bedazzled by the Crawfords' London assurance, and taking advantage of their father's absence, the Bertrams put on a play, complete with stage and green baize drapes. They choose *Lovers' Vows*, a sentimental melodrama that casts Maria opposite Henry Crawford (a great actor, naturally) and pairs Mary with Edmund. Anyone who's ever done any amateur dramatics will recognize the sexual tension generated in rehearsal and how a slick of greasepaint can go straight to the loins, and this is what happens.

Be inspired by the Mansfield Park players without the concomitant heartbreak and social degradation. If your home is too small for an in-house proscenium, join or start an amateur dramatic group. If that is impossible, why not just read a favorite play aloud together: you will find new depths in each other. Stage Struck is great for shy lovers who cannot say what they mean, but lose all inhibition once they are in character. It's also a good move for long-term couples who would like to make love to someone else in the safety of their own relationship. And don't stick with soppy melodramas. Just think who you could be: Stanley and Stella Kowalski (*A Streetcar Named Desire*), Amanda and Elyot (*Private Lives*)…

WELL-THUMBED CLASSIC   DRAMA QUEEN
♥ TRUE ROMANCE ♥ BODICE RIPPER HARDCORE (DEPENDING ON THE PLAY)
BREAK A SWEAT (IT'S HOT UNDER THOSE LIGHTS)

"What gentlemen among you am I to have the pleasure of making love to?"

THE MILL ON THE FLOSS

GEORGE ELIOT's novel, written in 1860, stars the luminous Maggie Tulliver, vibrant, passionate, intelligent, guileless, doomed, and often extremely irritating, and as much suited to life as a miller's daughter (which she is) as a bird of paradise in a hencoop. Her passion for books and the life of the mind, and obsessive (let's not go there) love for her oafish brother Tom, dominate her life. For instance, much to most modern readers' annoyance, Maggie submits to recalcitrant commands from her father and brother to sever her friendship with soul mate Philip Wakem, son of lawyer Wakem whom the Tullivers believe to be the architect of their ruin. Beneath all this flows the river, shaping Maggie's life and eventually taking it.

YOU WILL NEED

- ✿ A ROWING BOAT
- ✿ CUSHIONS
- ✿ A CLOAK
- ✿ A PARASOL
- ✿ ROSES (FOR TOYING WITH)

✿

~ FATAL ATTRACTION ~

After a troubled adolescence, Maggie grows up into a stunning young woman with the kind of deep, dark eyes a man could drown in, and goes to stay with her cousin Lucy Deane. She meets Stephen Guest, handsome, intelligent, agreeable, and Lucy's fiancé. They are magnetically attracted to each other—"Each was oppressively conscious of the other's presence, even to the finger-ends"—and the sexual chemistry between them is palpable. Nevertheless, they honorably resist it, parting forever after a passionate kiss on the towpath. The river, however, has other ideas, and a bend in the plot means that on a golden June day, Stephen and Maggie drift along the river alone in a rowing boat and a haze of desire; the tide pulls them farther than they meant to go, the dream is shattered, Maggie's reputation is shot, and Tom throws her out of the family home. After that it's all downhill.

Whatever the outcome for Maggie and Stephen, there is no denying that lust on a boat is very enjoyable. There is nothing quite so dreamily languid as floating down a river on a summer morning, "the breath of the young, unwearied day, the delicious rhythmic dip of the oars, the fragmentary song of a passing bird," the soft, rocking slap of water, the scent of passing meadows… aaah.

LOVE BOAT

This is good if your life is crowded with other people's demands, and you find it hard to be alone. Choose a clear day in early summer, rent a boat for two, take cushions, a blanket, and a parasol, and turn off your cell phone. Whenever Maggie and Stephen meet, half-open roses are mentioned—you could take a few with you, so you can strew the petals as you float downstream. Maggie and Stephen never do more than kiss, but don't feel that you have to stick so closely to the script. There is no need to renounce each other, just moor somewhere safe, preferably in the sun-dappled shade of some trees, and rock the boat. The novel ends in a heated rush, with Maggie drowning in a desperate and unsuccessful bid to save her brother from the floodwater. Don't let this happen to you.

"And they walked unsteadily on, without feeling that they were walking; without feeling anything but that long, grave, mutual gaze which has the solemnity belonging to all deep human passion."

MIDDLEMARCH

⟡

THE Great English Novel of the Nineteenth Century, *Middlemarch* (1871–72) is George Eliot's masterpiece, a study of the middle class of middle England, and what happens when individuals try to live epic, aspirational lives in a provincial landscape. At the center of the novel, the ardent, idealistic Dorothea Brooke, a St. Theresa without a cause, and the great-browed Dr. Tertius Lydgate, a man who wants to heal the world, orbit each other like the two components of a binary star. Although obviously an ideal match, they move on parallel lines and can never come together: Dorothea marries pompous elderly clergyman and scholar Dr. Edward Casaubon, a dry-as-dust empty husk whose life work *(A Key to all Mythologies)* has already been superseded by smarter brains; Lydgate falls for blonde, blue-eyed Rosamund Vincy, a beautiful bimbo with a shallow mind devoid of principle. The doctor goes supernova, burning out at fifty, a social success but a spiritual failure. Dorothea continues to gleam, her rays shining in a new direction.

> **YOU WILL NEED**
>
> ✿ ACCESS TO A LIBRARY
> ✿ STORMY WEATHER
>
> ✿

∼ WILL LADISLAW ∼

Some critics say Eliot is no good at romantic love, but show me a female reader who doesn't fall for Will Ladislaw the minute he appears. Delicious, impetuous, fervent Will Ladislaw, Casaubon's unlikely second cousin; wonderful, exotic, artistic Will, the boy with the gray eyes and the curly hair and the smile to die for, the unfettered Pegasus to Casaubon's hack. Toward the end of the book, Casaubon dies, various plot obstacles are gradually removed, and Will and Dorothea circle each other. Generations of readers, yourself included, silently scream, "Marry him!". Reader, she does.

BOOK LOVERS

Will and Dorothy finally come together in Casaubon's dusty library, their youth, beauty, and passion triumphing at last over dead letters. There is even a storm raging in case denser readers don't get the point. Why not consider an assignation in a library? The smell of old leather and learning and the hot muffled stillness of the stacks makes Book Lovers great for academic couples who have no quiet corners at home. Libraries have other lust advantages: big reading tables, ladders, sections where no one ever goes (try 001); and the discipline of silent sex can be very arousing. Avoid modern libraries with multimedia departments and cafés; you need old, established university libraries with agreeable proportions.

> "Her lips trembled and so did his. It was never known which lips were first to move towards the other lips; but they kissed tremblingly then moved apart."

WELL-THUMBED CLASSIC COME AS YOU ARE
♥ TRUE ROMANCE ☼ LANGUID (GOOD FOR MIDDLE-AGE LOVERS)

~ GETTING HIGH ~

There is nothing much more romantic than your lover appearing at your window three floors up, dramatically lit by a waxing moon. Julien's first ladder-borne foray (into Mme. de Rênal's room) was so successful that he later repeats the trick with Mathilde. This time he packs a pocket full of pistols, because he fears it may be an ambush, and Mathilde gets to ask him if that is really a gun in his pocket. You can play Ladder as either Julien and Mme. de Rênal (his Older Woman) or Julien and Mathilde (his Uptown Girl).

> ## "I ought to respond to her beauty. I owe it to myself to become her lover."

LADDER

Arrive an hour or so after midnight with a stout ladder and a handful of gravel. Throw gravel at your lover's window until she opens it. (Mme. de Rênal's window shutter has a heart-shaped hole in it, a perfect target.) Climb up and in, and fall into each other's arms. For authenticity, leave the light off, stroke each other, talk passionately for three hours and make love as the sun rises.

📖 A GOOD READ   👯 COME AS YOU ARE   🤼 LET'S PRETEND
💔 BODICE RIPPER   ✳ ATHLETIC (NOT FOR VERTIGO SUFFERERS)

EXTENDED LADDER

Mme. de Rênal is so thrilled that she hides Julien in the guest-room as a lust slave. The following night he has to jump out of the window, and she throws his clothes after him, but you need not go that far. At dawn, Julien hides in another room (Rênal) or a large cupboard in the bedroom (Mathilde). Your lover should bring you food and drink throughout the day (oranges, cookies, wine, coffee, soup, pie, bread) and you can start again in the evening.

> *"All genuine passion thinks of nothing but itself."*

Madame Bovary

~~~

Gustave flaubert's masterpiece of realist fiction (1857) was so real that the author stood trial for offenses against public morals (he was acquitted). Emma Bovary is literature's first desperate housewife, a silly, romantic fantasist shackled to a nice but dumb, unambitious, incompetent husband in a dull provincial town in northern France. Vain, restless, indulged, gullible, and discontented, Emma never gets over the fact that life is not like it is in the sentimental novels and girlie magazines she stuffs her pretty little head with. Emma is never satisfied: the grass is always *plus vert*, and whatever she's got, she wants something else, and as soon as she's got that, she wants what she has just scorned. A typical Pisces in fact…

YOU WILL NEED

✿ A HIRED CAR WITH DRIVER AND BLACKED-OUT WINDOWS
✿ A BUNCH OF VIOLETS (OPTIONAL)
✿ ACCESS TO A HORSE
✿ A RIDING KIT AND TRAVEL BLANKET

✿

~ love's fool ~

She takes lovers (professional womanizer Rodolphe Boulanger and callow lawyer's clerk Léon Dupuis), but fails to understand their motives or the basic rules of mistressing: she expects grand passion; they expect a free ride. A beautiful but manipulative little fool to the end, her last act before she dies in agony from self-administered arsenic is to look in her mirror. It's Flaubert's triumph to make the reader feel a sorrowful pang for such a flake. Because she lives in a small town full of prying eyes, Emma has to be inventive when plotting illicit rendezvous. While you don't have to act so dumb, or so adulterous, some of her moves may inspire you to find new ways and places to have fun. She occasionally meets M. Boulanger in Dr. Bovary's consulting room, so if either of you is a medical professional, you might consider making appointments and fitting your actions into an allotted time. Otherwise, why not try these:

FOREST RIDE

Emma's first tryst with M. Boulanger is a horse ride (for her health) to the noiseless depths of the local forest. She is so overcome at the sight of his supple leather boots, white worsted breeches, and long velvet coat that she cannot resist. Luckily, he has a blanket with him. You have probably already done this if you live in the country, but city types could take a weekend break and hire some unflappable horses.

> "The stuff of her habit clung to the velvet of his coat. She tilted back her white neck, her throat swelled with a sigh, and, swooning, weeping, with a long shudder, hiding her face, she surrendered."

DAWN RAID

Sometimes Emma got up before dawn, ran across the dew-soaked meadows to Boulanger's farmhouse, and slid in between his sheets smelling of fresh grass and clean air as the light turned to gold. This is excellent in spring and summer if you have a tight schedule; take it in turns to have a predawn run (don't get too sweaty) and come back cool and clean-limbed.

JIGGERY POKERY

Emma spends a long, hot afternoon rattling around Rouen in a closed carriage with Léon Dupuis. Flaubert does not tell us what they get up to, but the carriage bounces on its springs. It's her first sexual encounter with Léon, and he gives her a bunch of violets. Rent a car with darkened windows and a discreet chauffeur, and drive around your favorite city.

"She laughed a rich wanton laugh when the champagne frothed over the brim of her delicate glass and on to the rings on her fingers."

📖 WELL-THUMBED CLASSIC   🤸 🤸 LET'S PRETEND
♥ TRUE ROMANCE (EMMA THINKS)   💔 BODICE RIPPER (EVERYONE ELSE)
✪ BREAK A SWEAT

"The spectacle, so extraordinary
in a provincial town, of a carriage
with drawn blinds, continually
reappearing, sealed tighter than
a tomb and being buffeted about
like a ship at sea."

WUTHERING HEIGHTS

THE only novel written by Emily Brontë (the middle sister) was published in 1847; its author was dead a year later, when she was only thirty, after contracting tuberculosis, the romantic's disease of choice. E. Brontë was primarily a poet, and *Wuthering Heights* is steeped in poetic sensibility. Considered morbid and immoral at the time, it is now perceived as the first great Romantic Novel, uniting landscape, weather, intense emotion, and story into a tempestuous whole.

~ THE PLOT ~

Don't tell me you need the plot? Oh, all right. Starving street gypsy Heathcliff is brought to the Heights by kindly landowner Earnshaw, where he falls violently in love with Catherine Earnshaw. She loves him back just as fiercely, but marries local preppy Edgar Linton instead. Heathcliff runs away, but comes back to wreak dreadful revenge, usurping the family home and driving Cathy to her death; then he is haunted by her ghost until he dies eighteen years later and is buried in her grave. (He has already smashed open her coffin so that their bones can decay together.)

YOU WILL NEED

✿ WILD AND WINDY MOORS (PREFERABLY IN WEST YORKSHIRE, ENGLAND, BUT SIMILAR TERRAIN ELSEWHERE WILL DO)
✿ UNBRIDLED PASSION
✿ SENSIBLE BOOTS

✿

∼ OUR HERO ∼

Heathcliff is the archetypal dark, handsome, smoldering hero, who is fueled by the twin passions of love and revenge and knows only two speeds, ardent and psycho. However, no one could say he had a problem with commitment. Cathy is equally wild, harsh, and violent; this is not a story about bullies and victims. The obsessional love between Heathcliff and Cathy endures like the moors themselves, regardless of the weather raging above them; however cruelly they treat each other, they are joined at the soul.

∼ STORMY WEATHER ∼

Although a lot of the action takes place in the open, the atmosphere is strangely overheated, claustrophobic, and suffocating. As we are only ever at Wuthering Heights or Thrushcross Grange, the abode of the Lintons, the two families obsessively crossbreed as if there were no other gene pool in the county, and there are far too many women called Cathy. As he nears his death at the end of the book, Heathcliff's rage and anger abate like a dying storm, and you feel as if you have woken up from a febrile Gothic dream.

"In every cloud, in every tree, filling the air at night, and caught by glimpses in every object by day, I am surrounded with her image!"

WELL-THUMBED CLASSIC   DRAMA QUEEN

HARDCORE   ✸ ATHLETIC

HEATHCLIFF

This is very intense and atavistic, but makes a bracing change if you have been stuck in the bloodless, air-conditioned, antibacterial twenty-first century, drinking alfalfa-seed tea for too long. No special sex skills are needed to play Heathcliff—in fact, the more brutal and savage you are the better, so run across the springy moors until your legs twang, then tear each other's clothes off and get down to it; biting is allowed, and the whole experience is greatly improved if there are lowering storm clouds. Country lovers will find it easier than townies, who should take precautions. Think how embarrassed you will be if the Rescue Services have to be called out. And it's not a game for middle-aged lovers unless you are the kind of tough diehards who spend every weekend orienteering. If you want to go for the classic Heathcliff flowing white shirt look, for heaven's sake wear something sensible underneath; there's no shame in it—all-weather gear can be quite sexy, with all those zippers and hidden Velcro fastenings and secret map pockets.

"Whatever our souls are made of, his and mine are the same."

ANNA KARENINA

Tolstoy's novel (1875–77) is famously about unhappy families. These families are mostly made unhappy by inappropriate lust. At the center of the story is the adulterous passion between Anna, charming vivacious wife of the stiff and tedious bureaucrat Alexei Karenin, and the dashing Count Alexey Vronsky. (Note same first names: very useful in moments of passion.) Also steaming and throbbing ominously through the story is the unstoppable train; Anna meets Vronsky at Moscow station when she arrives to help patch up her charming, adulterous brother Stiva's crumbling marriage (irony, irony). When she returns to St. Petersburg, Vronsky contrives to be on the train so that he can meet her when it stops for a leg-stretching break. At the end, abandoned by husband, lover, and polite society, and in thrall to morphine, Anna throws herself under the train to die. The inspiration to draw from this tragic classic is not to embrace adultery, or throw your life away, but to have sex on a train. It was probably not Tolstoy's principal intention, but remember that the earth will always move, and it's a great way to spend time together.

YOU WILL NEED

✿ TRAIN TICKETS FOR A LONG WINTER JOURNEY
✿ A UNIFORM FOR VRONSKY (AVOID RAILROAD EMPLOYEE UNIFORMS—MAY CAUSE CONFUSION)
✿ FURS (FAKE) FOR ANNA AND VRONSKY TO HIDE BEHIND
✿ VODKA, CAVIAR, LEMON WEDGES (LONG JOURNEYS ONLY)
✿

"I can't think of you and myself apart. You and I are one to me."

RUSSIAN TRAINS

Trains and grand stations are romantic in themselves, and everyone understands the subtext of a great throbbing engine rushing into a tight, dark tunnel. Anyone can do it in a private sleeper car, and that's probably the best way to start, but take Anna's lead and be more adventurous; try it in the corridor, in open carriages, in the baggage wagon, etc. Match your rhythm to that of the train. Learn some suitable Russian words to cry out at significant times. You need not stick to the St. Petersburg–Moscow route, but it's more authentic to play Russian Trains in winter, when snowy landscapes rush past.

 WELL-THUMBED CLASSIC ♈ DRAMA QUEEN
♥ BODICE RIPPER ✪ BREAK A SWEAT (IF STANDING IN TRAIN CORRIDOR)

TESS OF THE D'URBERVILLES

A HEART-WRENCHING tale of doomed lust and passion, published in 1891—actually, all Thomas Hardy's tales are of doomed lust and passion. This one is also about decay and degeneracy—the decay of great names, the worm in the bud, the Alec d'Urberville-shaped snake in the grass. Hardy makes it all the more poignant for his favorite heroine by letting her enjoy a long, honey-drenched summer of love with her beloved before it all goes to hell in a haywain.

YOU WILL NEED

✿ A MILKING STOOL (OPTIONAL)
✿ ACCESS TO A DAIRY
HERD OR SUPPLY OF ORGANIC
WHOLE MILK AND CREAM
✿ A STRONG GRIP ON THE FUTILITY
OF EXISTENCE
✿ RIPE BERRIES

✿

~ A TALE OF WOE ~

Lovely, buxom, round-armed Tess goes to work as a dairymaid after the death of her illegitimate baby Sorrow, the result of the dastardly Alec having had his wicked way with her (this is Hardy, remember). Angel Clare, student-farmer and son of a preacher man, falls in love with Tess, entranced by the curve of her mouth and the taste of milk and honey on her skin. We know they are frolicking under the malignant blue glare of an Edward Hopper sky, because the plot conspires to prevent Tess telling Angel about Alec until their wedding night. As you know, it all goes horribly wrong, and Tess spends her last night of freedom sleeping on a sacrificial slab in the middle of Stonehenge before she is convicted and hanged for murdering d'Urberville. (Hardy was slightly too interested in hangings, especially of women; controlled constriction of the throat intensifies orgasm. Just a thought.)

"He likes 'ee best—the very best! We could see it as he brought 'ee. He would have kissed 'ee, if you had encouraged him to do it, ever so little."

~ RISING ABOVE ~

It has to be said that Hardy is a bit of a downer on the desire front. You probably don't feel at all in the mood now; what would be the point? We are all just maggots, whirling to our doom through uncaring space on a blighted planet that is but a rotten apple thrown by an ignorant boy. But if your heart is made of stronger stuff, you're not allergic to dairy products, and it looks like a fine summer, try Cream Tease—it's wholesome, it's organic, it's outdoors, and there is always plenty of hay around to roll in.

MODERN

LADY CHATTERLEY'S LOVER

D.H. LAWRENCE'S most notorious book was first published (privately, by him) in 1928. Naturally, the first printing sold out and it become an underground success. General readers were not allowed access to it until 1960, after a notorious obscenity trial, in which its literary merit was celebrated by solemn academics and serious writers. Today the sex scenes are considered a little risible, but hats off to Lawrence for writing so graphically about the subject; however we may splutter about the writing style now, and however butt-clenching the pubic flower-arranging scenes may seem, the book does contain much practical information and some novel locations for love in a cold climate. The essence of the adventures of Connie Chatterley and Oliver Mellors is that they take place outdoors—or at best in a shed. They do it in the road, they do it in the rain, they do it in the pheasant-rearing hut. So if your love life's getting stuffy, why not follow their example? Go commando, and constantly surprise each other while you are pruning the roses or out for a country walk.

YOU WILL NEED

✿ A ROUGH BROWN BLANKET
✿ A HANDFUL OF WILDFLOWERS
✿ PHEASANT CHICKS (OPTIONAL)
✿ A SHED
✿ OILSKINS
✿ ACCESS TO EXTENSIVE PRIVATE GROUNDS IS DESIRABLE, BUT A BACKYARD OR EVEN A PUBLIC PARK WILL DO
✿

"*She lay down under the boughs while he waited, standing there in his shirt and breeches, watching her with haunted eyes. Then he tore off his clothes and fell upon her. It was over soon, too soon and she could no longer force her own conclusion with her own activity... she clung to him unconscious in passion and he never quite slipped from her and she felt the soft bud of him within her stirring... he grew and unfolded within her and her body responded as it had not done before.*"

~ CHATTERLEY ROLE-PLAY ~

Most of the sex in *Lady Chatterley's Lover* is a straightforward variation on the missionary position. Mellors is almost always on top. It is the location and the natural ingredients (not to mention the class divide— posh girl and son of the soil) that provide the excitement. Of course, you have already read *Lady Chatterley's Lover* and know where the juicy bits are, but in case you have forgotten, here are the significant encounters to inspire you.

FOREPLAY

Connie feels the first pangs of lust for Mellors when she sees him washing in the backyard of his humble gamekeeper's cottage. You will need a pitcher and bowl of soapy water. Choose a warm day for this.

> *"He was naked to the hips, his velveteen breeches slipping down over his slender loins."*

PHEASANT HUT

Connie and Mellors first make love in the pheasant-rearing hut, but you can use an ordinary garden shed. Spread a brown blanket on the ground, and close the shed door so it is quite dark inside. Neither of you should speak. Mellors melts Connie's heart with his gentle handling of a helpless fledgling bird (you can hear the soft flap of the wings of a metaphor coming home to roost here), but it may be safer to play a background tape of chicks peeping.

> *"Then she quivered as she felt his hand groping softly, yet with queer thwarted clumsiness among her clothing."*

PHEASANT HUT WITH OILSKINS

A variation on Pheasant Hut; Connie should wait until it is almost night time, then go into the shed first, and sit on a stool in the doorway. Just before it gets too dark, Mellors strides up clad in wet oilskins. This is even more authentic if it is raining, but if it isn't, improvise with a pail of water. Continue as for Pheasant Hut.

> *"He hung up his gun, slipped out of his wet oilskin jacket and reached for the blankets. Then he sat down a moment on the stool and drew her to him."*

"*He* fetched columbines and campions and new-mown hay and oak tufts and honeysuckle in small bud. He fastened fluffy young oak sprigs round her breasts and in her navel he poised a pink campion flower and in her maiden-hair were forget-me-nots and wood ruff. And he stuck flowers in the hair of his own body and wound a bit of creeping jenny round his penis and stuck a single bell of hyacinth in his navel. 'This is John Thomas marrying Lady Jane,' he said."

A GOOD READ ✖ LET'S PRETEND ♥ TRUE ROMANCE
❂ BREAK A SWEAT (NOT FOR AGORAPHOBICS OR HAYFEVER SUFFERERS)

FLOWER ARRANGING

The outdoor life is not for everybody, and even Connie and Mellors occasionally met in his humble gamekeeper's cottage, so if you want to come in from the shed, consider Flower Arranging, a gentle postcoital exercise. Mellors decorates Connie and himself with wet wild flowers to symbolize their blossoming union (Connie is pregnant, but you need not be). You can substitute any of Mellors's choices with your own favorite flowers, but avoid large blooms, long, thick stems, and anything with thorns or prickles. Flower Arranging is very much a mood thing; one time it's wild and beautiful, the next you will be snorting with derision. It does require a certain naïve innocence, so is good for new lovers or for anniversaries when you are trying to remember what it was like to be new lovers. Try to synchronize moods though: if one of you is already feeling giggly, then sticking peonies in your delicate parts is not going to help.

WOMEN IN LOVE

Lawrence considered this, finished in 1916 but not published until 1920, his finest work, and cast himself as one of the four protagonists. It is the continuing story of Ursula and Gudrun Brangwen (from *The Rainbow*) and their fraught relationships with, respectively, Rupert Birkin (Lawrence) and Gerald Crich. Frankly, they are all insufferable, unpleasant, self-obsessed, arrogant show-offs, the first of the Me generation, but Lawrence is excellent on the love/loathe firing line between modern men and women, and if you want literary lust, you are spoiled for choice. Barely a paragraph escapes without mention of luminous white loins, melting into oneness, veins running with fire, soft blind kisses, and so on. It's intense, overwrought stuff on every level, with occasional endearing skids into bathos that always make you think of Mr. Salteena, Daisy Ashford's innocent class warrior in *The Young Visiters*.

YOU WILL NEED

✿ BRIGHTLY COLORED STOCKINGS
(FOR BOTH URSULA AND GUDRUN)
✿ BREAD, CHEESE, RAISINS, APPLES, CHOCOLATE
✿ AN OPEN-TOPPED CAR OR A PUNT (A SMALL, FLAT-BOTTOMED BOAT)
✿ A RESTLESS INTELLECT

✿

You have to be strong and tough for this one, sound in physical and mental wind and limb and prepared to get wet, cold, and a bit scratched about in the soul. Be ready to drop the odd Baudelaire reference into the conversation, speak scornfully in French if people laugh at your brightly colored tights, or break into German just to show off. There is a lot of rowing, canoeing, punting, swimming, walking, skiing, folk dancing, and tobogganing, as well as sex and the fight to the death for emotional dominance. The four spend a lot of time, alone and together, at Willey Water (yes, I know), where Gudrun first thrills to Gerald's white arc of a dive, the girls go skinny-dipping, and Ursula and Rupert share complicated kisses on the towpath.

Take your inspiration from Ursula and Rupert (the married couple groping toward soulful, emotional, and erotic equilibrium), Gudrun and Gerald (handsome, heartless, and dangerous), or even Rupert and Gerald (if you fancy a little bit of manly Japanese wrestling among the decanters in front of a roaring fire).

SECRET ENTRANCE

A Gudrun and Gerald inspiration: Gerald comes to Gudrun's house, sneaks in past all the family and into her bed in his muddy boots, and sneaks out at dawn. Don't plan in advance, just turn up. Great for bringing an edge back into a stale relationship.

> *"They threw off their clothes, and he gathered her to him, and found her, found the pure lambent reality of her forever invisible flesh."*

PUNT

An Ursula and Rupert inspiration; they take the punt over to a gloomy little willow-draped island, argue about the "utter ghastliness" of all humanity ("people are all balls of bitter dust"), eat chocolate and fall in love. You could replace the utter ghastliness argument with something more life-affirming.

> *"Oh, and the beauty of the subjection of his loins, white and dimly luminous as he climbed over the side of the boat, made her want to die, to die."*

I DROVE ALL NIGHT

Much more adventurous, and excellent for routine-huggers who want to let go. Ursula and Rupert enjoy a fine air-clearing row, then drive off into the sunset to Sherwood Forest (outlaw country), pausing only to buy a picnic and send a telegram to Ursula's father. They spend the night melting into each other beneath a rug underneath the moon and the fixed stars. Do the same, but send a text message instead.

"Her arms were round his neck, he kissed her and held her perfectly suspended, she was all slack and flowing into him, and he was the firm, strong cup that receives the wine of her life."

 WELL-THUMBED CLASSIC

COME AS YOU ARE (BUT WITH BRAIN IN GEAR AND NO CORPSING)

BODICE RIPPER ⚘ HARDCORE ✳ ATHLETIC

GERMINAL

THIS is not for everyone as it involves getting dirty, confined spaces, and the simulation of peril. Cerebral lovers may find it too gritty and realistic, but that was the effect Emile Zola was aiming for. *Germinal* (1885) is the thirteenth of Zola's ambitious twenty-book Rougon-Maquart series of experimental novels intended to explore nature vs. nurture and to analyze all aspects of life in Second Empire France. The experimental part meant throwing a bunch of characters into a well-defined social milieu and noting down what happens.

YOU WILL NEED

✿ A CAVE OR CELLAR
✿ COAL DUST
✿ MINERS' LAMPS
(OR FLASHLIGHTS)
✿ TIN BATHTUB (OPTIONAL)

✿

What happens is that, among other things, Zola's characters get horny. Yes, even *Germinal*, brutish though it is, is not short on lust, although you have to get through an awful lot about mining in northern France in the mid-nineteenth century first. How can there be desire in the hellhole that is Le Voreux mine? As the title suggests (Germinal is the seventh month of the French Republican calendar, namely March/April), life always thrusts through somehow, and the tender shoot that pierces the blackened ground of the main narrative (capital vs. labor) is the doomed love between the novel's protagonist, Etienne Lantier, and Catherine Maheu.

> "*Feeling her half naked body through her rags, so close to his, his virility returned and he took her.*"

COALMINER'S DAUGHTER

Trapped in the rising waters of the collapsing mine, Etienne and Catherine make love in an ultimate life-affirming gesture. Danger is a wonderful aphrodisiac, and Eros always stands up for life against Thanatos. Don't put yourselves at such risk, but re-create the atmosphere in your cellar; turn off all lights and heating, use flashlights sparingly, and find each other by touch. Consider rubbing coal dust on yourselves for social realism—it can be great fun soaping it off in an authentic tin bathtub afterward. Coalminer's Daughter can be adapted for potholers and speleologists, who might like to do it for real.

📖 A GOOD READ 🤸🤸 LET'S PRETEND
🕯 HARDCORE ☀ ATHLETIC (NOT FOR THOSE SCARED OF THE DARK)

NANA

ANOTHER in Emile Zola's Rougon-Macquart series, *Nana* (1880) is the story of Anna Coupeau, half-sister to Etienne Lantier (last seen down a mine), and, this being Zola, the embodied vengeance of society's wretched beggars and outcasts, a gilded fly spreading corruption from the dunghill to the drawing room. Arising from the gutters of Paris like Botticelli's Venus from the foam, Nana has a long mane of golden hair, alabaster skin, voluptuous hips, and a stupendous bosom. We first see her on the music-hall stage as the goddess herself. She has a voice that rasps like a chainsaw, but sex appeal by the wagon-load, and she instantly bewitches every man who sees her. Soon she is the most famous prostitute in Paris, thigh-deep in aristocratic lovers, jewels, money, fine clothes, apartments in the best arrondissements, etc. This sort of upstartery never goes unpunished; Nana dies horribly of smallpox, her face and body rotted and pustulent. However, she has some good times on the way, and you would be amazed at how many girls dream of being a sex goddess. Indulge your inner courtesan, dress in a bustier and velvet choker, and get your partner to play all your lovers in succession, from callow, white-gloved youths via fat bankers to minor royalty.

YOU WILL NEED

✿ A BOUDOIR
✿ A TIGER-SKIN RUG
(FAKE WILL BE FINE)
✿ A FULL-LENGTH MIRROR
✿ SATIN UNDERWEAR
✿ LAVISH GIFTS
(FOR LOVERS TO BRING)

✿

📖 A GOOD READ 🎭 DRAMA QUEEN 💜 BODICE RIPPER
🕯 HARDCORE ☼ LANGUID

MIRROR, MIRROR

Nana's overheated boudoir has red satin upholstery, a tiger-skin rug, and a full-length mirror. While her lover watched, Nana would stand before the mirror, let her clothes slide off, and revel ecstatically in her own beauty, caressing the slope of her pale, naked thigh, the curve of her bosom. Try it. And if you think the scenario is a bit clichéd, why not improve your languages at the same time and do it all in French?

> *"Her slightest movement fanned the flame of desire: the slightest twitch of her little finger could rouse men's flesh."*

THE GREAT GATSBY

F. SCOTT FITZGERALD'S 1925 masterpiece is a meditation on the hollowness of the American Dream, the heart-breaking fable of Jimmy Gatz who tightropes across the social divide only to immolate himself in Daisy Buchanan's incandescent green light. Almost everyone in it is superficial, dishonest, grubby-souled, and careless of other people, and Daisy, the unattainable princess with the voice full of money, literally gets away with murder.

Yes, but the clothes are gorgeous, and it's a great excuse for a party. Dress in pale linen suits and white crêpe-de-chine frocks, invite all your friends round, give yourselves ludicrous names (Clarence Endive? Mrs. Ulysses Swett? S. B. Whitebait?), and swap alluring lies and fantasies while swilling champagne from glasses larger than fingerbowls. We are never in on Gatsby and Daisy's love scenes, as the narrator tactfully removes himself, so you can do as you please, as long as you dress the part. Expensive clothes are very sexy; Daisy bursts into tears when she buries her face in one of Gatsby's huge collection of silk shirts. If the budget runs to it, rent a great cream-colored car coruscating with chrome, and roll around on its green leather interior, in a sea of dollar bills if possible.

YOU WILL NEED

✿ CASH IN LARGE AMOUNTS
(USE MONOPOLY MONEY
IF TIMES ARE HARD)
✿ A GREEN LIGHT
✿ A LARGE AMERICAN VINTAGE CAR
(OPTIONAL)
✿ PALE LINEN SUITS
AND WHITE DRESSES
✿ CHAMPAGNE
✿

GREEN LIGHT

Every night, Gatsby stares yearningly in the darkness across the small yet significant channel between East and West Egg at the green light at the end of Daisy's dock, so near and yet so far. Hang a green light at your window, or the end of the bed, and pine for each other for an agreed period. Dress in your best clothes, meet for tea at a mutual friend's house, and take it from there.

> "You always have a green light that burns all night at the end of your dock."

📖 UNPUTDOWNABLE   🏃🏃 LET'S PRETEND
♥ TRUE ROMANCE   ✪ BREAK A SWEAT (THE PARTYING REQUIRES STAMINA)

BRIDESHEAD REVISITED

WRITTEN while the world was at war (again), Evelyn Waugh's *Brideshead Revisited* (1945) is a long, slow, and yearning requiem for golden youth and uncorrupted love, shot through with desire, thwarted passion, and loss. Charles Ryder, only son of a chilly, loveless father, doesn't stand a chance against the pulverizing charm of the aristocratic Flyte family. He is bewitched first by the "magically beautiful" Sebastian, who transforms his life at Oxford, and then by Sebastian's sister Julia; as he passes a cigarette from his lips to hers (she is driving), he catches a "thin bat's squeak of sexuality, inaudible to any but him." It all goes wrong, of course— nothing ever stays that beautiful for long. Sebastian slides into alcoholism and Julia retreats into her barren marriage, but for languid luncheons and long, hot afternoons, where the sun stands still and the earth throbs to your own pulse, it can't be beaten.

YOU WILL NEED

✿ A FIRST-CLASS CABIN ON AN OCEAN-GOING LINER

✿ AN ENDLESS THIRST FOR PLAINTIVE NOSTALGIA

✿ CHARM

✿

PORT OUT, STARBOARD HOME

Charles and Julia, both married to other people, meet by chance on a transatlantic liner. A rainless storm rages (metaphor, etc.), but they finally consummate their desire at sunset amid the swell and chop of an angry sea. Book a cabin for two on a big ship and sail away; stormy weather (metaphorical or real) is not essential, but a bit of rough water can help improve a tired routine.

"*...now, while the waves still broke and thundered on the prow, the act of possession was a symbol, a rite of ancient origin and solemn meaning.*"

WELL-THUMBED CLASSIC   LET'S PRETEND ♥ TRUE ROMANCE
☀ LANGUID (NOT FOR BAD SAILORS)

FOR WHOM THE BELL TOLLS

B ASED on his experience as a journalist covering the Spanish Civil War (1936–39), *For Whom the Bell Tolls* (1940) is considered Ernest Hemingway's finest hour. It covers the last three days in the life of Robert Jordan, idealistic young American academic and explosives expert fighting with the Republican forces. As a clear-eyed look at how ideals melt away and love gets lost in the fog of war, it's hard to beat, but it's probably most famous for making the first literary link between human sexual activity and tectonic plate shifting. "Did the earth move for you?" Robert Jordan asks Maria after some epic action among the heather and pine needles of Castilla-León.

YOU WILL NEED

✿ COMBAT GEAR
✿ ACCESS TO A PINE FOREST
✿ A SLEEPING BAG OR BLANKET
✿ ACCESS TO A WAR ZONE
(ONLY FOR PROFESSIONALS)

✿

∼ IS THAT A GUN IN YOUR POCKET? ∼

Love and war have rarely been locked in so tight an embrace—not only does Jordan have a gun in his pocket, he is also very pleased to see Maria. There is nothing like the smell of TNT in the morning to make you want to assert yourself. Every time he looks at her, his throat goes tight, and there is rarely a moment when her small, round yet firm-pointed breasts aren't thrusting against her khaki shirt. It is amazing that the bridge the couple are trying to blow up doesn't spontaneously combust (if you're interested, the mission is botched and Jordan is left with a shattered leg to die a hero's death alone).

📖 WELL-THUMBED CLASSIC   🏃🏃 LET'S PRETEND (DEPENDING ON MILITARY STATUS)
🕯 HARDCORE   ❅ ATHLETIC (ONLY FOR THE YOUNG AND FIT)

VENUS AND MARS

Ideal for weekend warriors who don't want to sacrifice their sex life and girls who love boys who love guns. Dress up in combats, find a pine forest, get down, and give me twenty, soldier. Press your bodies lengthwise against each other and go at it until the earth moves.

> "*All was smooth with a smoothness and a firm rounded pressing and a long warm coolness.*"

ULYSSES

Derided by many in its day and censored for obscenity in the u.s and England, James Joyce's *Ulysses* was finally published in Paris in 1922. It's still sneered at as difficult, pretentious, and unreadable. So yes, it's loosely based on the adventures of Odysseus (page 12), and yes, it all takes place on Thursday 16 June 1904, and yes, it mixes anecdote, pastiche, journalese, playwriting, puns, in-jokes, stream of consciousness, myth, quotations, and word dancing, and yes, it doesn't always seem to make sense, and yes, there is no plot, but Molly Bloom's soliloquy is the best evocation of a lust-drenched summer afternoon spent in a hot bed alone that you will ever read. So one for the ladies, then.

Molly Bloom is Penelope to Leopold's Odysseus, and while he wanders the world, she spends her day in bed, weaving a fantasy of her past lovers. Her real lover, Blazes Boylan, has been visiting and she is in a rosy postcoital glow, drifting in and out of warm dreams, and recalling all the men she ever loved, while blissfully taking herself to her final, triumphant "Yes."

YOU WILL NEED

✿ A DAY OFF
✿ PAST LOVERS
TO DREAM ABOUT
✿ SEED CAKE

✿

MOLLY BLOOM

Clear the diary, lock the door, slip in between cool linen sheets, and abandon yourself to memories, fantasy, and bliss. You might want to bring refreshments—Molly eats seed cake as she thinks of her first time with Bloom. Purists will only do Molly Bloom on June 16th, but you might like it so much that you do it every Thursday.

"*And then he asked me would I yes to say yes my mountain flower and first I put my arms around him yes and drew him down to me so he could feel my breasts all perfume yes and his heart was going like mad and yes I said yes I will Yes.*"

UNPUTDOWNABLE

(OR UNPICKUPABLE, DEPENDING ON YOUR POINT OF VIEW)

COME AS YOU ARE (LITERALLY) ♥ TRUE ROMANCE ☀ LANGUID

FURTHER READING

Like all sensitive literary products, this is a slim volume, and thus cannot contain every trembling, passionate, inspirational moment to be found in Western literature. The examples we have given are from what are now accepted classics, but of course there is much more. Now you know how to do it, you can have fun finding your own arousing volumes, but below are listed a few more for you to be exploring. We have avoided works that just describe sex without a context (e.g. anything by Henry Miller, *Story of O*) as that would just be dull pornography, and left out distasteful stuff like *Les Liaisons Dangereuses* because, although full of lust, it is a tale of innocence corrupted and will make you sad rather than enthusiastic.

~ POETRY ~

If you are shy and don't enjoy role-playing or exertion, lying close and reading good poetry to each other can be very arousing. A selection of classic poets is given below.

Catullus (Gaius Valerius Catullus, 84–54 BC). Hot, itchy, lusty poet; smart lovers can read him in Latin.

Ovid (Publius Ovidius Naso, 43 BC–AD 17). Started it all with *Amores* (*Loves*) (10 BC) and *Ars Amatoria* (*The Art of Love*) (2 AD).

Sir Thomas Wyatt (1503–42). Brave poet and soldier, secret lover of Ann Boleyn. Try the middle verse of "They fle from me that sometyme did me seke", about an illicit midnight meeting.

William Shakespeare (1564–1616). *Love Sonnets*. Obvious really.

John Donne (1572–1631). The boss when it comes to seductive poetry; these feel as if they were written while he was in bed with his women, possibly while he was in action. "Oh my America, my New Found Land!"

Robert Herrick (1591–1674). One of the great celebrators of the female form, constantly inspired by his muse and mistress, Julia.

Andrew Marvell (1621–78). Author of what is still the most powerfully persuasive pick-up line in literary history in "To His Coy Mistress:"

> "*T*he grave's a fine and private place,
> But none I think do there embrace."

John Wilmot, Earl of Rochester (1647–80). Very clever filth from the pen of one of the world's great libertines. Dead at 33, having "blazed out his youth and health on lavish voluptuousness," but what a ride.

John Keats (1795–1821). Never quite got it on with his true love, Fanny Brawne, but *The Eve of St Agnes* will give you ideas for what to do on a winter's night.

W. B. Yeats (1865–1939). The Irish romancer; tread softly, for you tread upon his dreams.

e.e. cummings (1892–1962). American wordbender; try "she being Brand."

Pablo Neruda (1904–1973). Chile's national poet; try "Lone Gentleman."

~ NOVELS ~

Again a selective list, chosen because they are not only seductive but also have scenes that inspire.

Manon Lescaut, *Histoire du Chevalier Des Grieux et de Manon Lescaut* (1731) by l'Abbé Prévost. Sadly no room for this splendid example of all for love. Manon is a saucy wench, first seen grovelling very prettily in chains as she is about to be transported, who only gives up on her lover because he is poor. Swooning opera by Puccini, if you'd prefer to listen.

Narziss und Goldmund (1930) by Herman Hesse. Dreamy Jungian exploration of animus and anima (masculine/feminine), but Goldmund ("gold mouth") gets all the action. Arcadian ecstasy.

The Tin Drum (1959) by Günter Grass. Not everyone's first choice, but the seduction of Oskar's mother in the potato fields of northern Poland, and the trick with fizz powder in the belly button may appeal.

Ada (1969) by Vladimir Nabokov. Nabokov is of course most famous for *Lolita* (1958), which is also delicious but suspect, so *Ada* is recommended. You will need butterfly nets and a sundrenched attic. As with all Nabokov, it is really the language he uses to describe the curve of a cheek, the light on a mouth, that makes you come over all faint.

Perfume (1984) by Patrick Susskind. A *tour de force* evocation of scent that dizzies the senses and debones the limbs. Ghastly but gorgeous. Obviously, you will need perfume.

Love in the Time of Cholera (1985) by Gabriel García Márquez. For those who need convincing that there's life in the old dog yet.

Wise Children (1991) by Angela Carter. Deliciously entertaining, enchanting book with a description of lust at first sight that will melt your bones. It's about identical twins…

The Colour (2003) by Rose Tremain. Grim tale of New Zealand's nineteenth-century goldrush, made magical by the melting love affair, delicately consummated under the arching roof of a solid gold cavern.

INDEX

A

Alberto and Lisetta
17–19
Anna Karenina
see Tolstoy
Anonymous **see**
*Sir Gawain and the
Green Knight*
Arabian Nights, The 50–3
Ashford, Daisy
The Young Visiters 104
Austen, Jane 68–73
Mansfield Park 71–3
Pride and Prejudice
6, 68–70

B

balcony scene 44–5
Beaux Stratagem, The
see Farquhar
Boccaccio, Giovanni
16–19
The Decameron 16–19
Book Lovers 78–9

Brideshead Revisited
see Waugh
Brontë, Emily 88–91
Wuthering Heights 7,
88–91
Burton, Sir Richard
50, 58
Kama Sutra 50, 58
The Perfumed Garden
50, 58–9

C

Calypso's Cave 13
Chaucer, Geoffrey
6, 20–25
The Merchant's Tale
23–25
The Miller's Tale 20–22
China Cupboard 48–9
Classics 68–97
Claudine at School
see Colette
Cleland, John 34–7
Fanny Hill 34–7

Coalminer's Daughter
109
Colette, Sidonie-
Gabrielle
112–13
Chéri 113
Claudine at School
112–13
Congreve, William 46
Country Wife, The
see Wycherley
Cream Tease 96–7

D

Dawn Raid 86
Decameron, The
see Boccaccio
Defoe, Daniel 30–3
Moll Flanders 30–3

Dracula **see** Stoker
Dramatic Interlude 42–9

E

Earthy Romps 8–41
Eat Me 40
Eliot, George 74–9
   Middlemarch 77–9
   The Mill on the Floss
     74–6
Enkidu's lakeside embrace
   10–11
Exotica 50–65

F

Fair Persian Slave 53
Fanny and Will 37
Fanny Hill **see** Cleland
Farquhar, George 46
Fielding, Henry 38–41
   Tom Jones 38–41
Fitzgerald, F. Scott
   114–15
   The Great Gatsby
     114–15
Flaubert, Gustave 84–7
   Madame Bovary 84–7
Flower Arranging 102–3
Forest Ride 85
For Whom the Bell Tolls
   see Hemingway

G

Gawain **see** *Sir Gawain
   and the Green Knight*
   Gawain and the Green
     Lady 26–9
Genji, The Tale of **see**
   Murasaki Shikibu
Germinal **see** Zola
Gilgamesh, The Epic of 8–11
Golden Robe 60–1
Good Morning Little

Schoolgirl 112–13
Governor's Wife 56–7
Great Gatsby
   see Fitzgerald
Green Light 115

H

Ha Ha 71
Hamdonna and Bahloul
   59–61
Handy Nicholas and
   Alisoun 21–2
Hardy, Thomas 94–7
   Tess of the d'Urbervilles
     94–7
Heathcliff 91
Hemingway, Ernest
   118–19
   For Whom the Bell Tolls
     118–19
Highwayman and Harlot
   32
Homer 12–15
   Iliad 12
   Odyssey 12–15

I

I Drove All Night 107

J

Jiggery Pokery 86–7
Joyce, James 120–1
   Ulysses 120–1

K

Kama Sutra 50, 58

L

Ladder 82–3
Lady Bellaston 41

Lady Chatterley's Lover
   see Lawrence
Lawrence, D. H. 98–107
   Lady Chatterley's Lover
     6, 7, 98–103
   Women in Love 104–7
Ligeia **see** Poe
Love Boat 75–6

M

Madame Bovary
   see Flaubert
Maid and Master 32
Mansfield Park **see** Austen
Merchant's Tale,
   see Chaucer
Middlemarch **see** Eliot
Miller's Tale, **see** Chaucer
Mill on the Floss **see** Eliot
Mirror, Mirror 111
Modern 98–121
Moll Flanders **see** Defoe
Molly Bloom 120–1
Murasaki Shikibu, Lady
   54–7
   The Tale of Genji 54–7
Mysteries of Udolpho
   see Radcliffe

N

Nana **see** Zola
Nefwazi, Sheikh 58–61
   The Perfumed Garden
     58–61

O

Odysseus and the Sirens
   14–15
Odyssey **see** Homer

P

Pear Tree,
  Damyan and May
    23–5
Pemberley 69–70
Perfumed Garden **see**
  Burton; Nefwazi
Pheasant Hut 100–1
Poe, Edgar Allen 64–5
  Ligeia 64–5
Port Out, Starboard
  Home 116–17
Pride and Prejudice
  see Austen
Punt 106

R

Radcliffe, Mrs. Ann 66–7
  *The Mysteries of
    Udolpho* 66–7
rating system key 7
Rescue Me 66–7
Romeo and Juliet
  see Shakespeare
Russian Trains 93

S

Scarlet and Black
  see Stendhal
Scheherazade 50–2
Secret Entrance 106
Shakespeare, William
  42–5
  Romeo and Juliet 42–5
Sin-liqe-unninni
  see *Gilgamesh*
*Sir Gawain and the Green
  Knight* 26–9
Stage Struck 72–3
Stendhal 80–3
  Scarlet and Black 80–3
Stoker, Bram 62–3
  Dracula 62–3

T

Tess of the d'Urbervilles
  see Hardy
To Die For 64–5
Tolstoy, Leo N. 92–3
  Anna Karenina 92–3
Tom Jones **see** Fielding

U

Ulysses **see** Joyce

V

Vampyra 63
Venus and Mars 119

W

Waugh, Evelyn 116–17
  Brideshead Revisited
    116–17
Way of the World
  see Congreve
Women in Love
  see Lawrence
Wuthering Heights
  see Brontë
Wycherley, William 46–9
  The Country Wife 46–9

Z

Zola, Emile 108–11
  Germinal 108–9
  Nana 110–11

ACKNOWLEDGMENTS

Many thanks to professional storyteller Fran Hazelton for allowing me to use lines from her original version of the Enkidu and Shamkat episode from the *Epic of Gilgamesh* (page 10), soon to be published in her book *Stories from Ancient Iraq*.